Yachting
The History of a Passion

Robin Knox-Johnston

HEARST MARINE BOOKS
New York

First published 1990
© Phaidon Press Limited 1990
Text © 1990 Robin Knox-Johnston

Library of Congress Catalog Card Number: 90-81733
ISBN: 0-688-09991-2

Picture research by Philippa Thomson

Printed in England by Wm Clowes Limited, Beccles

Half-title: The crew climbing aloft to put their whole weight on the halliards to hoist sail.

Title page: The Isle of Wight provides the shelter that makes the Solent a natural amphitheatre.

Printed in England
First U.S. Edition
1 2 3 4 5 6 7 8 9 10

Acknowledgements

The publishers would like to thank the following for their kind permission to reproduce the photographs in this book: Mrs Harry N. Abrams Collection/© DACS 1990: 47; © Allsport: 118–9, 133, 136, 138, 142–3; © Allsport/Robert Hagan: 126–7; © Allsport/Trevor Jones: 149tr; © Allsport/Kos: 139–40; © Allsport/Steve Powell: 146–7, 148t, 149tl; © Allsport/Pascal Rondeau: 150–1; © Allsport/Oli Tennent: 135; © Allsport/Vandystadt: 122, 154; Ajax News & Feature Service: 2–3, 82–3, 100, 124, 130–1, 141, 145, 149b, 155, 157t; Beken of Cowes Ltd: 49, 65, 70tl, 78t, 93, 94b, 101, 105, 117, 121, 148b, 156; compliments of Bonhams: 64, 77, 102–3; The Bridgeman Art Library: 6–7, 10; The British Library, London: 1, 12, 15, 28, 29, 70tr, 72t, 99, 112c; Concepts Publishing Inc., Waitsfield: 106–7; Ian Dear, London: 61; Mary Evans Picture Library: 25t, 32t, 37, 41, 44t, 45b, 54, 56b, 66, 71, 73b, 78bl, 112t; Christian Février, Paris: 159; The Guardian: 164; Henri-Lloyd: 57c & b, 112b; Hulton-Deutsch: 39, 45tl, 45tr, 48, 52t, 56t, 68–9, 80, 108–9; Hydrographic Department, Taunton: 25b; The Illustrated London News Picture Library: 53, 57tl, 60, 79, 96, 97, 113t; London Transport Museum: 87; Mrs K. Long: 36; Lords Gallery, London: 110; Mansell Collection: 33; Reproduced by courtesy of the Trustees, The National Gallery, London: 10, 11; The National Maritime Museum, London: 8, 9, 13, 21t, 24, 32b, 50, 72b, endpapers; National Railway Museum, York: 86; The Observer Ltd./photo Jack Esten: 152b; Peabody Museum of Salem: 73t, 81, 152t; Pickthall Picture Library Ltd.: front cover, 20t, 114–5, 123, 128–9, 134, 144, 158; Popperfoto: 116, 137, 153t & bl; 157b, 160; Retrographic Archive Collection, London: 38, 74–5, 76t, 83b, 84tr, 92, 119, 163; all rights reserved, Rosenfeld Collection, Mystic Seaport Museum, Inc.: 94t (James Burton photographer), 166–7; Royal Exchange Art Gallery, London: 113b; Royal Thames Yacht Club: 14, 16, 17, 18, 22–3, 34–5, 42–3, 67, 76b; by kind permission of the Royal Thames Yacht Club/photos David Cripps: 19, 30, 31, 52b, 95; Royal Yacht Squadron, Cowes: 44b, 46t, 70b; The Hon. P.M. Samuel, London: 55; Sotheby's, London: 40, 46b, 51, 58–9, 84b, 85, 90–1; Sparkman & Stephens Inc./E. Levick: 94c; © S. & G. Press Agency Ltd: 104, 153br; the Tate Gallery, London: 26–7; courtesy of the Board of Trustees of the V&A: back cover, 111; Captain O.M. Watts, Piccadilly: 120; Windsor Castle, Royal Library © 1990 Her Majesty The Queen: 62–3.

Every effort has been made to trace the copyright holders, and we apologise in advance for any unintentional omissions.

Contents

1
The Birth of Yachting
(1600–1850)

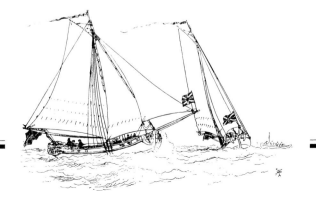

From its relatively casual beginnings some three centuries ago, yachting has developed to become one of the most highly sophisticated and competitive of modern sports. It started in the sheltered waters of the Netherlands with occasional cruises in contemporary work boats, limited to a day's sailing, and was introduced to Britain by the monarchy at the Restoration in 1660. The cruisers subsequently began to race, and this led to improvements in the design of yachts and developments in their rigging and sails.

The early races quickly emphasized the need for some form of handicap system. A yacht's speed is governed by her length, weight, the shape of her hull, and the amount of sail she can carry. In the past no two boats were ever built alike, so some method of adjusting all these factors had to be found in order to enable yachts to race on fair terms. Over the years handicap systems have become so complex that computers are now needed to calculate a yacht's rating and to ensure results reflect a good performance by the crew.

Yachting has also changed from being the pastime of the rich into an activity that is available to everyone. Huge yachts with their large paid crews are only the most glamorous part of the story. By the end of the nineteenth century, less wealthy people began to race in smaller boats, or in dinghies requiring only one or a limited crew, and, more recently, on windsurfers, which has become by far the most populous section of yachting. The range of the sport is enormous, encompassing not only competitive day sailing in large and small boats, and long-distance sailing across oceans in yachts that may be either single-handed or with crews of twenty or more, but also the vast core of people who just enjoy cruising with family or friends. The sport of yachting is now so wide and diversified that it may fairly be described as 'athletics on water', the one common bond between all the participants being that they require some type of boat.

A yacht has been variously described as a vessel used for sport, leisure or state ceremonies. In the latter context the earliest yacht in existence is the barge, 133 feet (40.57 m) long, discovered in a pit at the base of the Pyramid of Cheops in 1954. This vessel, dating back to 2,600 BC, was found in 'kit form' and in a remarkably preserved condition. It has subsequently been assembled, but its precise function is not clear.

Previous page: Dutch ships at Dordrecht in the eighteenth century, by Hendrick de Meyer.

SEYLENDE YSSCHUYT

A typical Dutch ice yacht of 1620, which was probably a working boat with leeboards removed.

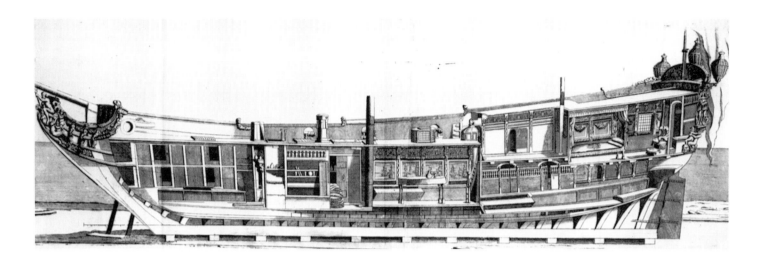

A 1693 engraving by V. Coronelli showing a cutaway of the cabin arrangement at the time.

Possibly it was the Pharaoh's funeral barge, or it was for use in his afterlife, however, it does demonstrate the Egyptians' capability, nearly 5,000 years ago, of producing quite large vessels for purposes other than war and trade. The barge is now housed in its own museum at the foot of the Pyramid.

Throughout history famous people have owned leisure boats, although they might have had additional roles when required. Cleopatra presided over the battle of Actium on a state barge. The remains of a very large galley were found in 1932 in Italy when Lake Nemi, near Rome, was drained. The Nemi ship, destroyed during World War II, measured 235 feet (71.68 m) in length and had a beam of 110 feet (33.55 m). In northern Europe, Athelstan, King of England, was given a vessel with purple sails by the King of Norway in AD 925, and a hundred years later Hardecanute, King of Denmark and England, owned a large vessel requiring eighty rowers. The merchant states of Italy had sumptuous craft for grand occasions, as did the growing maritime powers on the European Atlantic coast. Elizabeth I of England, in addition to owning state barges, was presented with a small yacht, the *Rat of Wight*, built in 1588, a diminutive version of the sailing ships of the period. In 1604, Prince Henry, eldest son of King James I, had a small craft made by Phineas Pett at Chatham to teach him the basics of navigation. Named the *Disdain*, she weighed 30 tons and was still in the Navy list in 1618.

During the sixteenth century, the inhabitants of the Netherlands across the North Sea were in revolt against their ruler, King Philip II of Spain. Their country, low lying, split by rivers and canals, was ideal territory for waging war in small boats, and a fast sailing vessel was developed for this reason. These boats were called *jaghts*, from the Dutch word for hunt or chase, and they were small, lightweight, fast warships. As the Netherlands slowly won its independence, and simultaneously became Europe's premier maritime nation, vessels of this kind evolved for communication and commercial work. They were also used by prosperous burghers, who employed them in the same way as the coach and horse in less aquatic countries. By the middle of the seventeenth century the *jaghts* were a familiar sight around Holland, and racing between rival boats had advanced beyond a competition between two that happened to be in close proximity, into a more formal affair.

Yachting, as the sport was swiftly named, did not spread elsewhere until the Restoration of Charles II of England in 1660, when the Dutch East India Company presented the king with the yacht *Mary*. She was reported to have cost £1,300 to build, a large sum in those days. King Charles had spent much of his exile in Holland, and had shown a keen interest in the sport, so the gift was appropriate. The *Mary* resembled a miniature

A shipping scene with a Dutch yacht firing a salute, painted in 1665 by Jan Van de Capelle.

Opposite: A typical coastal scene on a calm day, by Van de Velde.

man-of-war, and she carried eight guns and required a crew of thirty. The king was so delighted with her that within a few months of his accession he ordered another yacht from British shipwrights, which was adapted for the deeper waters of England. This was followed by four more within the next three years, commissioned either by the king or by his brother James, Duke of York. During the remainder of his life the king is said to have owned at various times not less than twenty-eight such vessels.

Not unnaturally, a degree of rivalry developed between the two brothers, and the earliest documented sailing race in England took place in 1661, when they raced their respective craft from Greenwich to Gravesend and back. The duke won the outer leg, the king the return. The wager, according to the diarist John Evelyn, who accompanied the king, was for £100:

> October 1st 1661. I had sailed this morning with his Majesty in one of the yachts or pleasure boats, being very excellent sailing vessels. It was on a wager between his other new pleasure boat, built frigate-like, and one of the Duke of York's; the wager one hundred pounds sterling; the race from Greenwich to Gravesend and back. The King lost in the going, the wind being contrary, but saved stakes in returning.

Royal enthusiasm for ships and yachts led to experiments for their improvement, and in 1663 a 'Double Bottom' ship designed by Sir William Petty was sent by Lord Massereene in Dublin to the Royal Society in London for evaluation. (Double bottom in this context does not refer to an inner lining to a single hull, but to a catamaran with two hulls or bottoms.)

Multihulls, as their name implies, are boats with more than one hull. There are three basic types: the two-equal-hulled craft, known as catamarans, from the Tamil words *Kattu Maram*, meaning 'tied logs'; the proa, which has two hulls, a main one and an outrigger used for balance; and the trimaran, which has a central hull and outriggers on each side. The Polynesian seafarers of the Pacific Ocean were the first people to

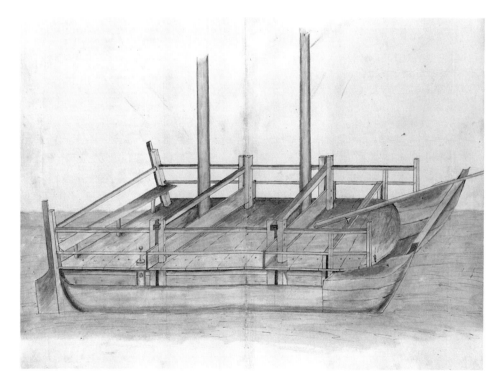

William Petty's efforts to produce a boat with a shallow draft and large sail area led him to design a double bottom ship or catamaran.

The royal yacht *Mary* arriving at Stade in Holland in 1761 to collect Queen Charlotte and take her to England.

employ multihulls for long-distance voyages. Early European explorers noted that their catamarans, made with primitive tools and constructed by sewing planks of wood together with rope, could be found all over Polynesia, and were capable of undertaking voyages as long as 2,000 miles (3,700 km). The largest of these craft measured over 60 feet (18.3 m) in length.

William Petty's ship was found to have a considerable speed advantage over conventional vessels, but it was eventually lost at sea and interest in the catamaran type died for 200 years. All the early yachts in England were built on the lines of miniature men-of-war and were not primarily intended for racing. The principal activity of these early vessels seems to have been to manoeuvre in the fashion of war fleets, even going so far as to fire at each other with their small cannons, fortunately loaded with blanks. Charles and James soon had personal fleets of supporters, co-ordinated on naval lines, with an Admiral, Commodore, Rear-commodore, and so on, and this naturally transferred to yacht clubs when they were created.

Royal patronage declined after James II was expelled in 1688, and although subsequent monarchs owned yachts, they were reserved for state occasions until the reign of George III in 1760. However, the sport did not die, and in 1720 the first yacht club in the modern sense was formed by a group of wealthy individuals in Ireland. Called the Cork Water Club, it is still thriving as the Royal Cork Yacht Club. Membership was limited to twenty-five, meetings took place every spring tide, and the Admiral was not allowed to bring more than two dozen bottles of wine to his treat! Its claim to be the oldest yacht club in the world has been challenged recently by Russian historians,

The Cumberland fleet racing at Blackfriars on the River Thames in 1782.

Opposite: Flags were the earliest form of identification at sea. Almost the first action of a new club was to design a distinctive burgee.

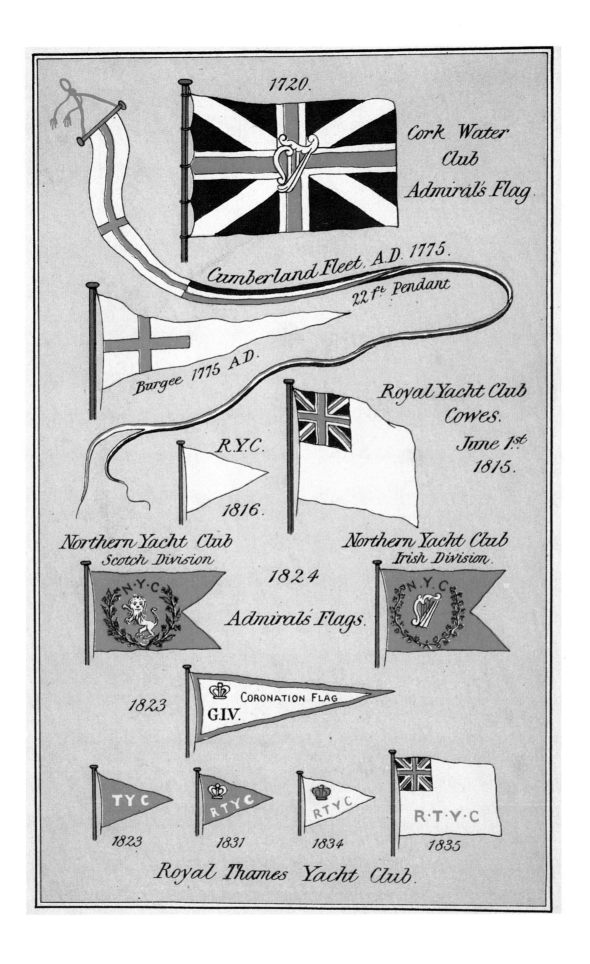

1720.

Cork Water Club Admiral's Flag.

Cumberland Fleet, A.D. 1775.

22 f.t Pendant

Burgee 1775 A.D.

R.Y.C. 1816.

Royal Yacht Club Cowes. June 1st 1815.

Northern Yacht Club
Scotch Division

Northern Yacht Club
Irish Division.

N.Y.C.

N.Y.C.

1824

Admirals Flags.

1823

CORONATION FLAG
G.IV.

TYC
1823

RTYC
1831

RTYC
1834

R·T·Y·C
1835

Royal Thames Yacht Club.

who maintain that Peter the Great founded the Flotilla of the Neva in 1718 specifically for sail training. Yachts were also already a familiar sight in New York harbour by 1717. In England, the earliest yacht club appeared at Starcross in Devon in 1770.

During the eighteenth century, the Industrial Revolution led to growing prosperity, and rich merchants began to acquire yachts to vie with the aristocracy. Initially they enjoyed cruising in company, speed was not essential, and tidiness in manoeuvres was considered to be more important. However, as numbers grew, owners became competitive, and in 1749 the first recorded race between more than two boats was held, on the Thames between Greenwich and the Nore. It was won by the *Princess Augusta*, which, as a foretaste of things to come, had been specially built for the occasion. By 1775 racing was quite common on the Thames, and during that year the Duke of Cumberland put up a twenty-guinea silver cup for a race which led to the foundation of the Cumberland Sailing Society, the forerunner of the Royal Thames Yacht Club, whose headquarters are in Knightsbridge, London. The club's racing rules, the first to govern the sport, included one that stated that the owner must steer his boat, and that his crew could not exceed three people. A year later there are accounts of yachting regattas – the word is Venetian in origin – at Cowes, then the major town on the Isle of Wight, favourably situated close to Southampton and in the middle of the sheltered waters of the Solent.

The change in emphasis from cruising to racing led to a radical development in the type of yacht being constructed, as owners pressured shipwrights to design faster boats. The swiftest small craft around the coast were the cutters used by both smugglers and revenue agents, and these were modified for yachting. The Cumberland Society

Racing on the Thames attracted considerable attention in the early Victorian era as this advertisement for a spectator boat shows.

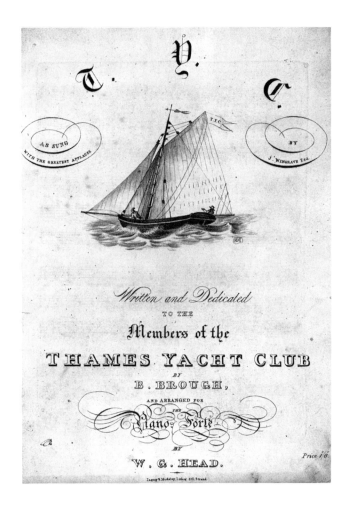

Yacht clubs not only had flags and clubhouses, but also their own songs.

soon had a large fleet of these yachts competing regularly on the Thames between Black-friars and Putney. Some of their owners cruised when they were not involved in regattas, and in 1777 one of the society's yachts, the *Hawke*, whilst sailing in the English Channel, was chased by an American privateer and had to flee into Calais. Incidents of war and piracy meant that those early days of cruising held risks that would discourage most of today's yachtsmen. Racing itself was hardly less hazardous, and physical conflict between the crews was not unknown when the boats came too close to each other. For example, in 1795 the crew of the *Vixen* boarded the *Mercury* armed with cutlasses, and cut away her rigging!

In 1812 an official regatta took place at Cowes, by then a very popular summer base for yachtsmen, which three years later was to lead to the establishment of a new aristocratic club, the Yacht Club, under the chairmanship of one Lord Grantham. In 1817 the Prince Regent joined, followed by his brothers the Dukes of Clarence and Gloucester. When the Prince Regent became King George IV in 1820, the club changed its name to the Royal Yacht Club. In 1824 the club moved to a house on the foreshore at Cowes, and in 1829 it was granted the privilege of flying the white ensign. Only four years later it was renamed again as the Royal Yacht Squadron. Although some nations have separate ensigns for merchant ships and warships, only the British have a choice of three: the white used by the Royal Navy; the red flown by merchant ships; and the blue used by Fleet Auxiliaries and ships with Naval Reserve crews. (The colours are based on those used to denote the original rating of British admirals, the red being the Senior Admiral, followed by the white and blue.) British yacht clubs to this day employ all

and its clubs spread rapidly to the British colonies; racing was taking place in Tasmania in 1831, and in 1838 the Royal Hobart Regatta Association came into existence. That same year the Royal Southern Yacht Club was established near Southampton in England, and in 1843 the Royal Harwich was formed, a year before the Royal Mersey and Royal Bermuda. The records of the Royal Bermuda proudly claim credit for the first international yacht race, between their *Pearl* and the American *Brenda*, won by the former. In the United States, yachting was proliferating. The New York Yacht Club was founded in 1844, although there had been regular races between yachts from New York City and Boston for some time before this date. The inaugural meeting of the club was held aboard the *Gimcrack*, the fifth yacht owned by its first Commodore, John C. Stevens.

Elsewhere, the Segel Sallskabet, which became the Royal Swedish Yacht Club, was founded in 1830, and France's first club, the Societé des Regates du Havre, in 1840. The Dutch, although largely responsible for creating the sport, did not have a club until 1846, when the Koninklijke Nederlandsche Jachtclub (the Royal Yacht Club of the Netherlands) was formed. In the same year the Imperial Yacht Club of St. Petersburg was established in Russia. The latter acted as host to Britain's Royal Yacht Squadron in 1847, in a competition for a gold cup presented by the Czar.

Yachtsmen the world over continued to be drawn from a wealthy elite, the owners perhaps taking the helm, but leaving the other work to large crews of professionals. Wagers between owners continued, but cups, usually of silver, were becoming common for races involving more than two boats. Naturally any owner who gambled large sums on his yacht's ability against others demanded ever faster boats from the builders. In general, the cutter was still the favoured rig in European waters, where the British had set the fashion, but across the Atlantic in the United States yachting was evolving independently, and the schooner was more popular. Although some owners had sailed aboard yachts when visiting in either Europe or America, no direct comparison of the two styles of craft could be made until a yacht crossed the Atlantic and raced against the opposition on the other side. However, no one could have predicted that, when they did meet, it would lead to one of the most famous and long-lasting of all sporting competitions – the America's Cup.

In 1851 Britain was at the height of her imperial power and prosperity, and to display this to the world a huge exhibition was held in a specially erected building, the Crystal Palace in London. It was understood that Britain's Navy ruled the waves, and her yachtsmen were confident that they had the finest yachts and sailors. As a part of the exhibition, it was suggested that one of the New York pilot boats, renowned for their speed, should sail to the Thames and demonstrate her ability when racing against British yachts. Following an exchange of letters between the Earl of Wilton, Commodore of the Royal Yacht Squadron, and John C. Stevens, his opposite number at the New York Yacht Club, the venue for the competition was changed to Cowes, and an American syndicate built a yacht, the *America*, which sailed across the Atlantic to take on the best British yachts of the day.

On 1 August 1851, the *America* arrived off the Isle of Wight and was met by the British yacht *Lavrock*. An impromptu race developed which the *America* won handsomely. This performance had an undesirable effect as far as Stevens and his syndicate were concerned, as they had hoped to recuperate some of their costs by betting on the organized races, but after beating the highly rated *Lavrock* so convincingly, takers were hard to come by. Without a bet the Americans refused to race, but were prevailed upon by one of their party to remain until 22 August to participate in the Squadron's Around the Isle of Wight Race for a hundred-guinea cup presented by Queen Victoria. Their entry was accepted by the Royal Yacht Squadron, who also generously altered their usual rules to allow the *America* to boom out her sails. (At the time, sails had

Commodore Stevens, one of the owners of the *America*, and a founder and first Commodore of the New York Yacht Club in 1844.

Previous page: A typical race scene by J. M. W. Turner of Cowes Regatta in 1827; the yachts are beating to the west.

The distinctive front to the New York Yacht Club building in 44th Street, New York.

to be set out on one side only, which was a disadvantage to a schooner when running down wind as the aftermost sail blanketed the forward ones.)

Rules for racing had existed since the eighteenth century, based mainly upon those for commercial traffic. As racing became more cut-throat, extra precautions had to be taken to avoid collisions. There were already rules relating to the rights of a vessel with the wind behind her over one sailing close to the wind, and a vessel on starboard

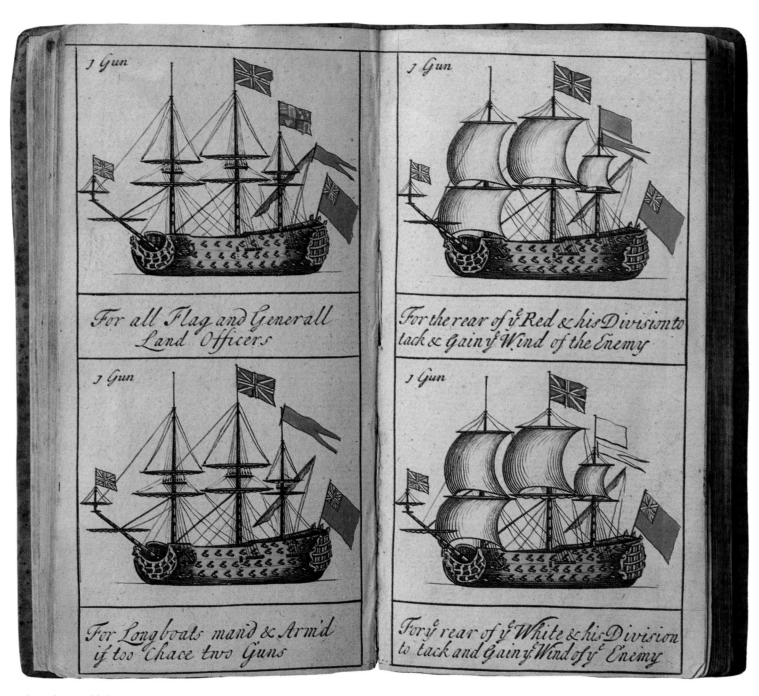

'The sailing and fighting instructions or signals as they are observed in the Royal Navy of Great Britain', 1741. They would have been used to govern the early yacht club manoeuvres.

Opposite: The seventh annual cup presented by the Duke of Cumberland in 1781, and the first cup to be presented for an open yacht race.

tack to another on port tack. Further rules were now added to cover which craft had right of way when two were approaching a buoy together, or how far a boat being overtaken could block one behind her. In many cases these were discussed and agreed before each race, but gradually a generally accepted set of rules was adopted – although they were not necessarily always obeyed, as we shall see.

The press gave the Around the Isle of Wight Race good advance coverage, and a huge crowd flocked to Cowes for the race, which was to start at ten o'clock in the morning. The fifteen competitors were anchored off Cowes in two lines, eight cutters in one, and seven schooners, including *America*, in the other. As was customary, at the five-minute preparatory gun the yachts began to hoist sails, and at the start-gun weighed their anchors and got under way. The *America* was the last to leave the anchorage, but within a very short time had taken the lead, and held it to the finish.

The arguments continue as to whether the *America* was the fair winner of the race, but the facts support her. For some reason, she failed to go round the Nab Tower, a mark of the course, but she was not alone in missing it. There is little doubt that she was balked as she ran through the home fleet. But her two main British competitors, *Arrow* and *Alarm*, withdrew when the former went aground and the latter went to her assistance. Only the much smaller *Aurora* hung on gamely, and finished a mere eight minutes behind the *America*, but the race rules gave victory to the first boat to cross the finish line, without any consideration of size or handicap. The story goes that when Queen Victoria enquired who won, and on being told, asked who was second, she was informed that there was no second. This anecdote probably arose because of the situation at the Needles, three-quarters of the way round the course, when *Aurora* was eight miles astern of *America*. But the wind went light towards the end of the race, which enabled *Aurora* to make up a lot of ground. Both yachts finished after nightfall.

Within a week the *America* had been sold to Lord John de Blaquiere for £5,000 (about $20,000), and her owners returned home with a profit. They left behind hurt pride amongst the aristocrats of yachting, and confusion and concern throughout a whole nation, which felt that its security, which depended upon supremacy at sea, had been badly exposed. The race was seen as a triumph for the schooner over the cutter rig, and schooners suddenly became the vogue. (It was really more of a victory for high quality sailmaking, as the *America's* sails were cut much flatter than the baggy English ones.)

The America's Cup.

The *America* under construction in New York in March 1851, from the *Illustrated London News*.

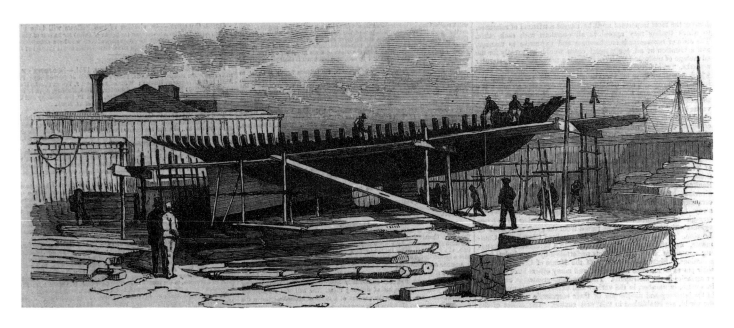

The *America* with her sails boomed out. Usually this was not allowed in British racing at the time, but the visitor was the exception.

The hundred-guinea cup, which was shared amongst the original syndicate for a year, soon became known as the America's Cup. In 1853 it was presented by the syndicate to the New York Yacht Club, who offered it as a permanent challenge, under a deed of gift dated 8 July 1857, for yacht clubs of any nation, on the understanding that the Cup itself would be held by the winning club, and not by the owner of the winning boat, a rule that applies today. Unfortunately the American Civil War intervened before any challenges were made.

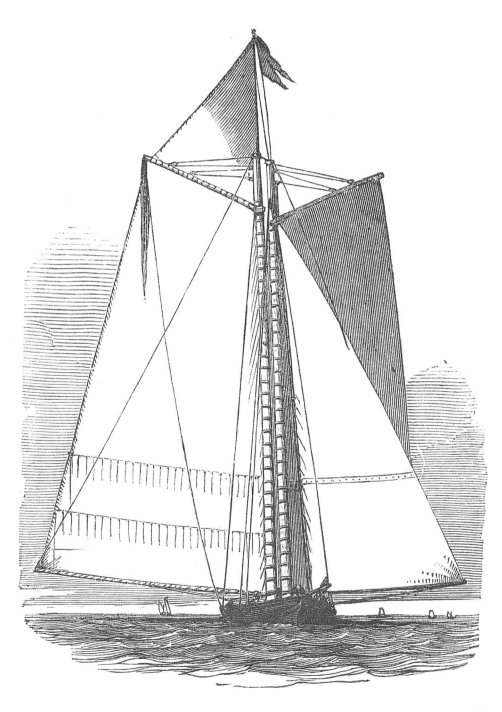

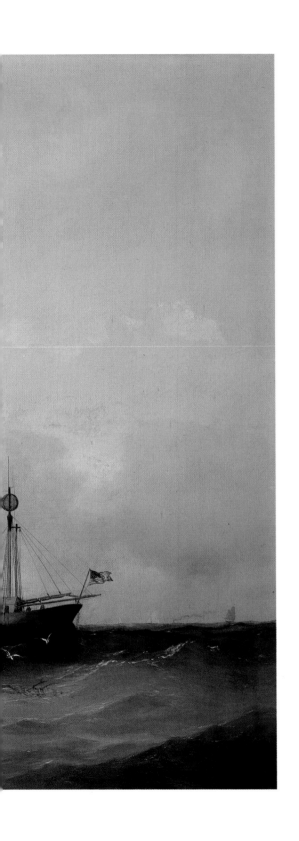

2
The Patrician Years
(1850–1890)

The publicity and attention given to the *America* did much to promote yachting in Britain, America, and Europe. Many countries, such as Spain, Germany, Portugal, Belgium and Denmark, saw clubs being founded in the next decade. Italy was one of the last to join the fashion in 1879, with the Yacht Club Italiano.

In Britain, design features of the *America* were copied, waterline entries became hollow, and bows were given a rake. Schooners became popular, and one owner, Thomas Bartlett, even built a replica of the *America* and named it *Sveridge*. By 1854, although there were 511 cutters in British ownership, the number of schooners had risen to 138, with yawls totalling seventy-five. The next twenty-five years have been contemporaneously described as the apogee of the sailing yacht, and possibly this was true for the grand yachts. Over thirty large schooners and an equal number of cutters were racing regularly, and towards the end of the period the big yawl was establishing itself as a favoured rig. One of the best-known yawls was the 126-ton *Jullanar*, designed and built near Maldon in Essex by E.H. Bentall, an agricultural implement maker. Her success, which included being the leading racing yawl in 1877, and achieving the best record of any English boat in 1878, was probably due to her fine underwater lines, which were considered to be a breakthrough in design at the time. Sails also received their fair share of attention, with the introduction of more tightly woven cloth and sails being laced to the booms instead of loose-footed as had been the British custom prior to the arrival of the *America*. Perhaps the most long-lasting innovation was a sail used by the *Sphinx* which was full and lightweight and set when running dead before the wind. The name of the sail was corrupted by the sailors to spinxer, but it has come down to us as the spinnaker.

Ocean racing began in 1866 when three American schooners raced across the Atlantic. This event was repeated regularly as a feeder for American yachtsmen coming over for the European yachting season. American businessmen were quick to appreciate that yachting had caught the public's interest and that therefore it could be valuable for advertising a product. In 1866 they launched the first of what we would call a sponsored sail, when the *Red, White and Blue*, an experimental lifeboat with 'Ingersolls Improved Metallic Lifeboat' emblazoned along her topsides, made the journey from the United

Previous page: *Cambria* winning her race across the Atlantic in 1870 against the American yacht *Dauntless* before her unsuccessful challenge for the America's Cup.

The Royal Irish Yacht Club

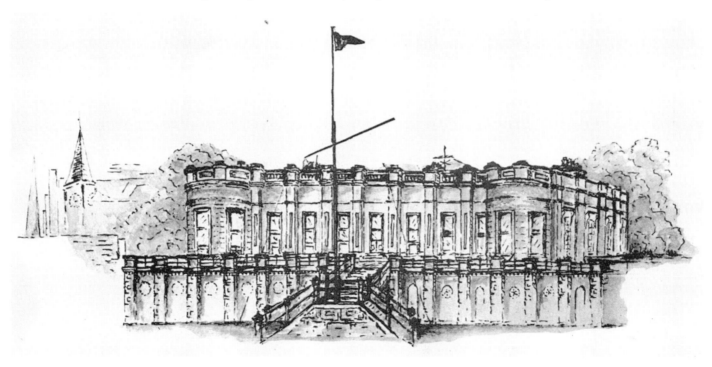

The *Little Western* and her crew, George Thomas and Fred Norman, who crossed the Atlantic in 1881.

States to England. An additional appeal was that the skipper, William Hudson, undertook the voyage single-handed. The venture obviously attracted notice and may well have brought its sponsors commercial success, as the boat was exhibited in London and Paris, and the log was published as a book, one of the earliest in yachting's now enormous literature.

William Hudson's solo journey was not the first. In fact the first solo Atlantic crossing had been eighty years earlier, in 1786, when an American citizen of British birth, Josiah Shackford, sailed from Bordeaux to Surinam. Little is known of Shackford's adventure, perhaps because at the time long voyages in small boats by survivors of shipping losses were not uncommon. Indeed, only three years later Captain William Bligh sailed 3,600 miles (6,675 km) across the Pacific Ocean in a small open launch with eighteen men after the mutiny aboard HMS *Bounty*.

Further solo passages were made in both directions across the Atlantic. 1870 saw a voyage from east to west by an American, John Buckley, in a converted ship's lifeboat, the *City of Ragusa*. Alfred Johnson, a Grand Banks fisherman, sailed from Gloucester, Maine, to Wales in 1876. Even more dramatically, Bernard Gilboy set out from British Columbia for Australia in 1882, and was rescued the following year in an exhausted condition when only 160 miles (296 km) short of his objective. Gilboy spent 162 days alone at sea, and his food ran out some time before his rescue. He survived by eating anything he could catch, and even ate the barnacles on his boat.

So in addition to establishing the first transatlantic races for fully crewed yachts, Americans may also claim to have invented long-distance short-handed oceanic sailing (by which is meant sailing with a crew of one or two). It was not until 1881 that a Briton, Frederick Norman, with one crew in his 16-foot (4.88 m) cutter *Little Western*, crossed from London to the United States.

Meanwhile shorter-distance single-handed cruising was gaining popularity. The first voyage of note occurred in 1855, when a Reverend Hughes sailed from England to the Baltic in his 8-tonner *Pet*. The pastime was given added impetus by the publication in 1869 of R.T. McMullen's famous book *Down Channel*, an account of the author's cruises along the coast of England; and in 1870 of E.E. Middleton's *The Cruise of the Kate*, detailing his solo voyage around Britain. The fact that these authors could manage

Belgium thread labels *c.*1900.

Opposite: The music for the Royal Yacht Club's waltzes, published in 1861.

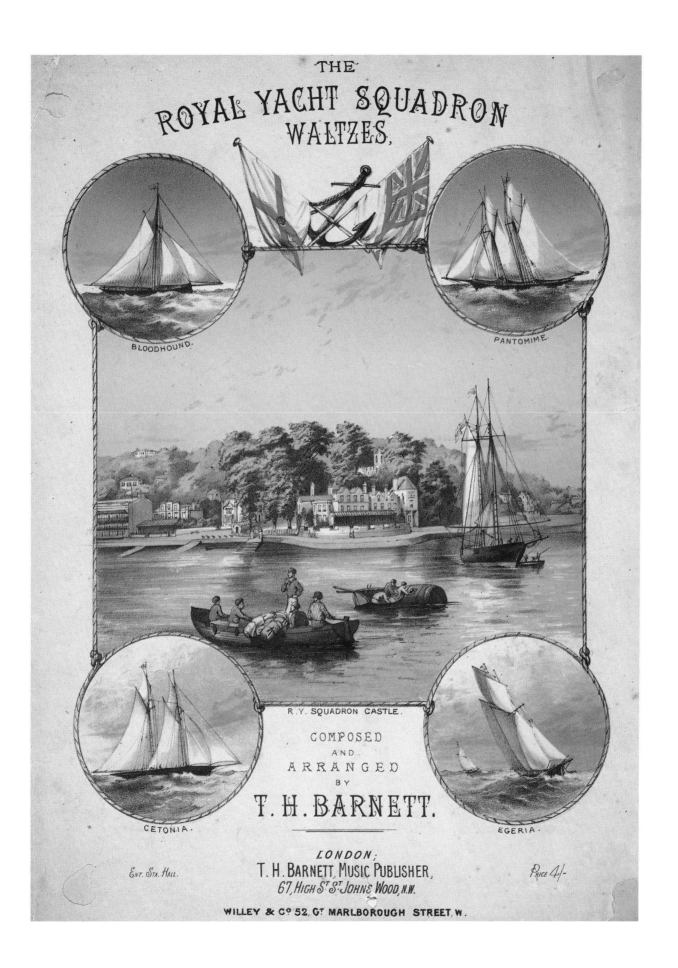

THE
ROYAL YACHT SQUADRON
WALTZES,

BLOODHOUND.

PANTOMIME.

R.Y. SQUADRON CASTLE.

COMPOSED
AND
ARRANGED
BY
T. H. BARNETT.

CETONIA.

EGERIA.

LONDON;
T. H. BARNETT, MUSIC PUBLISHER,
67, HIGH ST ST JOHNS WOOD, N.W.

WILLEY & Cº 52, Gt MARLBOROUGH STREET, W.

ENT. STA. HALL.

Price 4/-

their boats competently on their own, and thoroughly enjoy the experience, excited others, and a number of craft built just for single-handing followed, both for inland and offshore use.

An expansion of private cruising in comparatively small craft commenced at this time. The Cruising Club was established in England as early as 1880, and became entitled to the prefix Royal in 1902. This club still has no permanent home, its members feeling that their boats, rather than a clubhouse, should be the focus of attention. Few people exemplified the pleasures and freedom of cruising more eloquently than Edward Knight, who bought his first boat, a yawl named *Ripple*, whilst in his early twenties. In 1880, at the age of twenty-eight, he and some friends acquired a larger yawl, the *Falcon*, in which they cruised and explored the Amazon. Later, he converted a ship's lifeboat, also named the *Falcon*, and visited the Baltic. His various books about his adventures, *The Cruise of the Falcon*, *The Falcon in the Baltic* and *Small Boat Sailing*, were widely read.

An English nautical writing box of *c.*1880, the lid veneered with a seascape scene of two ketches.

As yachting was now being taken up by the middle classes, the broadening of its appeal led to a number of experiments with boat types as well as rigs. During the 1800s there was a variety of multihulls built. One of the first multihulls in the yachting sense had been *Double Trouble*, built in 1820 for Commodore Stevens of the *America* syndicate. In 1868 John Mackenzie of Belfast had a 21-foot (6.4 m) catamaran built for use in shallow waters. Known then as a Double Boat, it featured a large chest amidships, which could be flooded with 1,780 lbs (805 kgs) of water to provide ballast in heavy weather. H. Melling of Liverpool built a similar vessel for the River Dee in 1873.

The great American designer Nathaniel Herreshoff produced a number of catamaran designs in the 1870s which proved exceedingly fast. One, *John Gilpin*, 32 feet (9.27 m) overall and weighing 3,300 lbs (1,500 kgs), was clocked at 14 knots on a reach and could make $6\frac{1}{2}$ knots when sailing close to the wind — an omen for the future! However, when the multihulls began to show a speed advantage, they were quickly outlawed by conventional yachtsmen, who, then as now, disliked being beaten by boats that cost less and went faster.

Meanwhile, the America's Cup gathered dust until 1870. Part of the problem was that the British had been badly shaken by their defeat in 1851. British yachts had been described as tea chests when compared with the *America*, and no one was prepared to challenge until yacht design in Britain had closed the gap on the Americans. *Hunt's Yachting Magazine* was only expressing the view of many when it printed, 'Surely when little Clyde-built cutters of 25 tons can accomplish the voyage to Australia it is not too much to expect that our leading yacht clubs would organize a fleet of powerful schooners to cross the Atlantic and wake up Uncle Sam in the Bay of New York'. Eventually, the Vice-Commodore of the Royal Harwich Yacht Club, James Ashbury, wrote to the New York Yacht Club and challenged for the America's Cup with his yacht *Cambria*. He asked for a match race between two boats in open water. He also requested that centreboarders be excluded.

A protracted correspondence about the rules commenced and continued until the race. In 1870 *Cambria* sailed across the Atlantic, beating a fast American yacht, *Dauntless*, in an informal race by one hour and forty-three minutes, which filled the Americans with apprehension. After further wranglings, the first and only race of the challenge itself took place on 8 August off New York. Far from it being a match race between two yachts, *Cambria* found herself up against eighteen opponents. And although it must be admitted that the *America* had been balked once by the British in her race in 1851, *Cambria* was put about by the American yachts no less than six times when she was on starboard tack and, then as now, had right of way under the racing rules. Ultimately this led to a collision in which *Cambria* lost some rigging and her fore topmast, and she finished eighth.

Opposite: Afternoon tea under difficulties.

Overleaf: *Livonia* crossing the Atlantic to make the second challenge for the America's Cup, 1871.

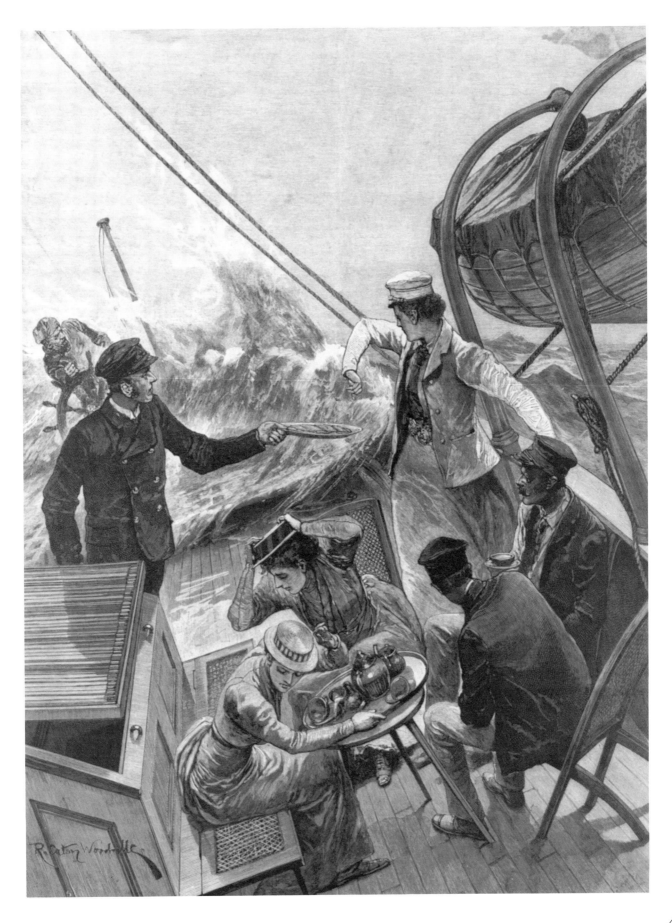

Cowes

Cowes was originally a small village on the Isle of Wight, at the mouth of the River Medina, which empties into the middle of the Solent opposite Southampton Water. The town, which is divided into east and west by the river, owes its foundation to the establishment by Henry VIII of two coastal defensive forts in 1540. It rapidly developed as the Isle of Wight's main port.

Yachting regattas commenced because of the comparative shelter offered to small boats by the Solent, and in 1815 the Yacht Club moved to the town. With the rise of this exclusive club, which became the Royal Yacht Club in 1820 and the Royal Yacht Squadron in 1833, the town became the centre of yachting in Britain. The Squadron continues to be housed there on the site of the western castle, which provides a superb view of the Solent and an excellent starting platform for races, perhaps the most notable being the Fastnet Race.

The Cowes regatta is still the premier yachting event in Britain and takes place during the first week in August each year. The regatta became a part of the social season during the nineteenth century when Queen Victoria bought nearby Osborne House, and it endures as one of the social events of the year. The British royal family supports the occasion, and the royal yacht, together with her attendant guard ship, are a familiar sight anchored just off the town in the roads. There is racing every day, with balls and other parties laid on in the evenings. The week culminates in a giant fireworks display on the Friday night.

For yachtsmen the real attraction of Cowes Week, as the regatta is called, is the excellent and exciting racing, which spans the whole spectrum of yachting, from small day boats to the largest Maxi ocean racers, and draws competitors from all over the world.

Cowes Castle, the clubhouse of the Royal Yacht Squadron.

Members of the Royal Yacht Squadron in 1895, with the Kaiser the odd man out with a white cap cover. The lady in white below the battlements is reputed to be Mrs. Langtry.

The battery of starting guns at the Royal Yacht Squadron being loaded in 1912.

Crowds waiting by the Royal Yacht Squadron steps in 1909.

Cowes illuminated for the annual fireworks display in 1904.

Raoul Dufy's painting of the interior of the Royal Yacht Squadron.

Opposite, above: A painting of yachts in front of the clubhouse of the Royal Yacht Squadron.

Opposite, below: The Cowes waterfront in 1936 showing the Gloucester Hotel and Royal Yacht Squadron.

The Royal Yacht *Osborne* in Osborne Bay in 1857.

The Sleeping Saloon on the Royal Yacht *Osborne*.

The Pavilion and Dining Room on the Royal Yacht *Osborne*.

The main saloon of *Galatea*, which lost an America's Cup challenge to *Mayflower* in 1886, illustrates the luxurious accommodation in racing yachts at the time.

Ashbury took his defeat in good part and entered another challenge soon afterwards, although he threatened to take legal action against the New York Yacht Club regarding the definition of the word match. The club put the problem to the only survivor of the original donors of the America's Cup, George L. Schuyler, who confirmed that in his view a match meant a race between just two boats. Thus reassured, Ashbury pressed on with his challenge and built a new boat, *Livonia*, launched at Cowes in 1871. However, the New York Yacht Club demanded the right to field any one of four defenders, thus gaining the advantage of selecting the right boat for a particular day's weather.

The contest was to be the best of seven races. *Columbia* defended and won the first and second, and lost the third. The New York Yacht Club selected *Sappho* to defend the fourth and fifth races, and she easily won both. However, Ashbury claimed that the second race of the contest should be rerun, as there had been a misunderstanding about the rules. General opinion in America supported his request, but the New York Yacht Club declined and the series ended in disarray. Ashbury returned to England, saying that he would challenge again, but that next time he would bring a lawyer, thereby establishing a tradition still associated with the Cup!

Although the British were discouraged by what they considered to be American foul play, the America's Cup was now established as an important trophy and in a few years it became the premier international yachting competition.

The next challenge for the Cup was made five years later in 1876 by the Royal Canadian Yacht Club of Toronto, on behalf of Major Charles Gifford. This time the New York Yacht Club agreed to nominate only one defender, but the challenger, a schooner called the *Countess of Dufferin*, arrived in New York with no time for a work-up and was beaten in two straight races by the American *Madelaine*. A second Canadian challenge was undertaken in 1881 by Alexander Cuthbert, the leading shareholder in the *Countess of Dufferin*, but his new boat *Atlanta*, as unprepared as her predecessor,

The American defender *Mischief* leads against the Canadian challenger *Atlanta* in the 1881 America's Cup series.

Aveyron, winner of the Prince of Wales Challenge Cup in 1874.

A graphic illustration of a flying start in 1874.

was defeated as easily by *Mischief* (owned by an English member of the New York Yacht Club, J.B. Busk – so the only time the British have ever won a Cup series it has been in the role of defender!).

Atlanta differed from the previous challengers in that she was a cutter. Development in this type of yacht had come a long way since 1851, and, in particular, the 45-foot (13.73 m) Scottish-built cutter *Madge*, when visiting American waters, proved almost unbeatable despite her small size, and impressed the Americans with her design. From now on cutters began to replace schooners in major racing everywhere.

Following the 1881 America's Cup series, which had scarcely been a contest, the New York Yacht Club determined to avoid the event developing into a farce, and they returned the Cup to George L. Schuyler, asking him to re-present it with a new deed of gift. There were two major alterations to the second deed: the challenging club had to hold its annual regatta on an ocean (which effectively disbarred a club on the Great Lakes); and no one who had challenged could do so again until after someone else or until after two years had elapsed. What did not go unnoticed in Britain was that the new deed also specified that there should be only one defender. After a gap of fourteen years during which no British yacht took part in the contest for the Cup, the Royal Yacht Squadron entered a challenge in 1885 on behalf of one of its members, Sir Richard Sutton, and his yacht *Genesta*.

A typical Victorian starting gun, belonging to the Royal Thames Yacht Club.

The fifth and sixth Cup series in 1885 and 1886 were both lost to American yachts yet again – *Genesta* was defeated by the cutter *Puritan*; and a year later the English yacht *Galatea* lost to *Mayflower*. Although the results were disappointing from the British point of view, both series did much to raise the integrity of the competition, and they were exceptional insofar as they were not conducted in a blaze of publicity or in a welter of lawyer's letters. (Reading an account of the history of the America's Cup, it is perhaps hard to understand just how intense a match race can become. Any small advantage that can be gained by manipulating the rules is seized, and inevitably tempers become frayed as each side feels that the other is going beyond the bounds of good sportsman-

ship. Add to this the fierce nationalism of the Americans, and the miracle is that any races take place at all.)

The Royal Clyde Yacht Club came forward as the seventh challenger in 1887, with a G.L. Watson design, *Thistle*. Watson had been to America to study their yachts, and he shrouded his own design in secrecy while he was building the boat. However, when *Thistle* came to be measured, the challenge was almost refused, as it was found that her waterline was nearly 2 feet (.6 m) longer than estimated in her original application. But the New York Yacht Club need not have worried. *Volunteer*, their chosen defender, won handsomely. The Scots complained that the course favoured local knowledge, but this seems petty now: the challenger should have arrived in America in good time for practice. After all, the *America* could have claimed a similar disadvantage in 1851.

Before the next challenge the deeds of gift were altered yet again and a pause ensued whilst the new rules were absorbed. The general opinion in Britain was that there were now so many conditions that the Cup was unwinnable.

Whilst the America's Cup attracted the major publicity, a quiet revolution was taking place at the opposite end of the sailing spectrum. Small sailing dinghies, cheap to build and requiring only one or two crew, were becoming more popular. Dinghies had been employed as tenders to large vessels and as work boats around the coastlines of many countries, and they were easily adapted to recreational use. In the 1850s the Americans had been racing a version of the New York watermen's *Sandbaggers*, a broad shallow-draft vessel which set an enormous sail area, with a long bowsprit jutting forward of the

The start of the Jubilee Yacht Race in 1887.

A lady in naval rig, from *The Album*, 1895.

James Tissot, *Boarding the Yacht*, 1873.

Fashion Afloat

Fashion aboard yachts has inevitably owed more to practical considerations than to the designers of haute couture. Small boats are exposed, and the sea and spray are regular visitors, so the premier requirement has always been to keep dry and warm rather than to cut a dash. Oiled canvas coats and sou'westers, those sensible hats traditionally worn by fishermen and lifeboatmen, were the normal wear for early yachtsmen.

However, on large yachts, when the weather permitted, the owners and skippers adopted a style of dress based upon naval uniforms. White duck trousers and a black reefer jacket with a modified naval officer's cap became the accepted rig during the nineteenth century, and continues to be worn in some smart circles today, but more usually as a shoregoing outfit. The crew's clothing depended upon the fads of the owner. Some also sported the naval style, whilst other crews had a version of the fisherman's serge trousers and heavy sweater. To this day various clubs retain their own uniforms, such as the mess jackets worn by members of the Royal Yacht Squadron.

As yachting was enthusiastically taken up by society during the nineteenth century, ladies inevitably joined their husbands for the social events, living aboard the larger yachts or ashore in hotels. On fair days some took part in the races as well. Initially they wore the same clothes as they might expect to use on dry land, and their cumbersome fashions meant that in rain or rough weather they were quickly forced to take cover in the saloon. Despite the handicap of their long dresses, however, they began to sail in special races, but it must have been a relief when ideas changed after World War I and allowed them the freedom of comfortable trousers or slacks.

Nowadays the sailing gear worn afloat is generally informal, more practical and less restrictive, but with its own changing fashions. Open-necked shirts or T-shirts have replaced the lace blouse or stiff collar and tie. Colour and cut have found their place even in foul-weather gear, which takes the form of waterproof overall trousers and jackets, with designer boots and shoes for footwear. Most professional crews wear a distinctive, colourful uniform, usually with their yacht's name embroidered on the shirts. Shore attire is often a smarter variation of the sailing rig, but in the evenings ladies in long party dresses still have a problem if they are living on a boat and the ferry to the beach is a small rubber dinghy.

A party aboard Prince Henry's launch at Kiel in 1912.

King Edward VII with a party of fashionably dressed visitors aboard *Britannia*.

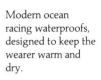

Modern ocean racing waterproofs, designed to keep the wearer warm and dry.

Deck-grip sail boots made by Henri-Lloyd.

Yacht racing, American style, on the Delaware River in 1883.

Previous page: *Grayling*, a typical schooner, leading a race in 1888.

The captain and crew of the *Volunteer*, winner of the 1887 America's Cup series.

boat and a bumkin sticking out aft. They relied on bags filled with sand for ballast, which had to be shifted around quickly by the crew of six to eight when the boat tacked. They began to disappear in about 1880 when improved dinghy designs arrived, but they were to be found in Australia until the 1960s. The American *Cat-Boat* also evolved as a dinghy at the same time. This was very broad-beamed – sometimes the beam was half the length – and, with a shallow draft, relied on a centreboard to prevent leeway (the drift of a boat downwind). The rig was distinguished by a mast placed in the bows of the boat, which set a gaff sail. The *Una*, a typical $16\frac{1}{2}$-foot (5.03 m) *Cat-Boat*, was brought over to Cowes in 1852, and her name was subsequently used to describe any single-sailed boat with a mast stepped in the bow.

In Britain small work boats were also modified, and in due course finer and lighter copies of traditional designs were produced. Different areas had their favourite models, such as the *West of England Conference* dinghy, which attracted followers in the Torbay area and had a class association by 1889. In East Anglia the Yare and Bure Sailing Club had the *Norfolk* dinghy. Another dinghy was the *Waterwag*, whose class association was created in 1887. The original design specified that two men should be able to carry it across the pebble beach at Shankill, County Dublin. At only 13 feet (3.97 m) long, 4 feet 10 inches (1.47 m) broad, with 75 square feet (6.97 sq m) of fore- and aftsail and a 60 square foot (5.58 sq m) spinnaker, the class became very popular. It grew rapidly around Dublin Bay and then spread further afield, even as far as India. At the class's centenary regatta in Dublin Bay in 1987, representatives attended from the Royal Madras Yacht Club.

Dinghies were cheap to build and easy to handle (a hundred years ago a new *Waterwag* cost £15, and sails were £2-£3, depending upon whether they were cotton or silk), and they enabled the sport to draw further away from its traditional wealthy roots. New clubs sprouted up wherever the sailing conditions were suitable.

W. Wyllie
May 25th Britannia & Valkyrie

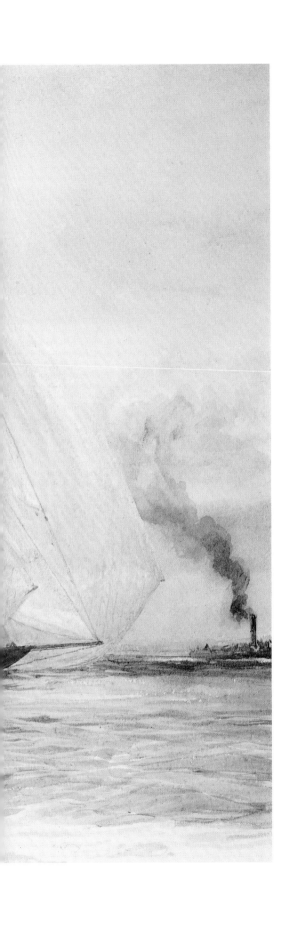

3
The Golden Age
(1890–1914)

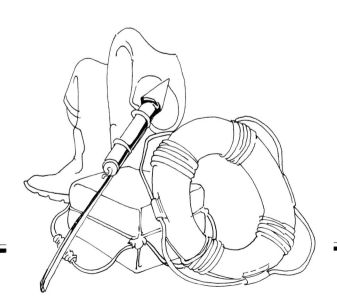

The high costs of building and upkeep of large boats maintained yachting's reputation as an elitist sport, a reputation that to a certain extent it still has today. Towards the end of the nineteenth century though, the general appeal of cruising and racing led to an increase in the production of smaller, cheaper vessels. These required few or no professional crew, and allowed the less affluent to participate. A new system of rating yachts introduced by Dixon Kemp, a naval architect and one of the founders of the Yacht Racing Association (later to become the Royal Yachting Association), led to the appearance of many yachts known as Raters (see pp.162–3), and also aided the proliferation in smaller yachts. The Americans had developed a comparable rule, and in 1895 the Minima Yacht Club offered a challenge trophy for yachts measuring to the English half-rater formula. This was won by *Ethelwyn*, of the Seawanhaka Yacht Club, believed to be the earliest yacht in the United States to use a Bermudan mainsail. The next logical step in yachting evolution was the development of the One-design classes, where all the boats in a class were of exactly uniform dimensions and had equal sail areas. The idea spread from America, where one of their most notable yacht designers, Nathaniel Herreshoff, was responsible for a range of One-design classes for the New York Yacht Club, measuring from 30 to 70 feet (9.15 to 21.35 m) in length. One-designs have the advantage that everyone can see exactly how a race is progressing, and the first boat to cross the finish line is the winner. This avoids complicated calculations to decide the outcome.

Sailing was included in the modern Olympic Games established by Baron de Coubertin in 1896, although the only two 'international' yachting competitors were Scotland and England. At the second games in 1900, more nations participated in the sailing events, with three gold medals being won by Britain, while France took two, and Germany and the United States took one each. It has continued as an Olympic sport ever since, although the boats have become progressively smaller.

Adventure sailing remained newsworthy, particularly the Atlantic crossings by single-handers. On 17 June 1891, two Americans, Josia Lawlor and Bill Andrews, set out from Boston to race each other across the Atlantic in their 15-foot (4.58 m) yachts, for an agreed wager of £1,000. Andrews was picked up shortly after departure, but Lawlor arrived near Land's End in Cornwall, after a passage of forty-three days. This must be seen as being the first single-handed transatlantic race.

Four years later another American set out alone from Boston on what was to become one of the most famous voyages in yachting history. Joshua Slocum was a Master Mariner who fell on hard times in middle age (see p.152). He was finally left with the remnants of an old 37-foot (11.29 m) gaff sloop named the *Spray*, which he rebuilt. He intended to sail alone around the world, but people hearing of his plan said that his boat was unsuitable. However, Slocum paid no heed, commenting wryly that his severest critics had never even crossed the Gulf Stream, and implying that they did not know what they were talking about. He sailed from Brier Island in Nova Scotia bound for the Azores on 2 July 1895, a voyage of eighteen days, and after a short stay proceeded to Gibraltar. He had intended to go through the Mediterranean and the Suez Canal, but warnings of pirates persuaded him to alter his plans, and he chose to head west for Cape Horn instead. He had various adventures, the most famous being the occasion in the Magellan Straits when, on being boarded by barefoot Patagonians intent on theft or worse, he sprinkled his yacht's decks with tin-tacks.

When he entered the Pacific, Slocum slowly sailed to Australia, where he remained for some time, cruising the coast, lecturing, and refitting his boat. He then made a classic run of 2,700 miles (5,000 km) in twenty-three days to the Cocos Keeling Islands in the Indian Ocean, during which time he touched the helm only once. His next major stop was in South Africa, where President Kruger informed him that, since the world

Previous page: Britannia and *Valkyrie* in 1893.

The menu card for the Temple Yacht Club's 35th annual dinner in 1892. The Prince of Wales, shown astride Pegasus, was the guest of Baron de Rothschild.

The saloon of Sir Thomas Lipton's *Erin*, which he lived aboard whilst attending regattas.

The dining room aboard the *Semiramis*.

The German Kaiser's yacht *Meteor,* 1894.

Latona, a nineteenth-century watercolour by Barlow Moore.

was flat, he could not have sailed around it, only around its edge! Slocum set out again after giving more lectures, and, avoiding Spanish warships as he neared home (America was at war with Spain), he finally anchored at Newport, Rhode Island, on 27 June 1898.

Slocum's book, *Sailing Alone Around the World*, is one of yachting's greatest classics and a magnificent sailor's yarn. He made no further long voyages, but cruised south each winter to the Caribbean and returned to New England for the summer. It was on one of these passages in 1909 that he disappeared, possibly run down in the dark by a ship, as he had a dislike for the smell of paraffin, and refused to show a running light at night.

The cult of small boat sailing had been strongly promoted in the 1860s by the Englishman R.T. McMullen, a keen supporter of what he called 'Corinthian sailing' as opposed to 'Cowes yachting' – he preferred sailing to socializing. McMullen maintained that a well-found small vessel, if properly handled, was safer at sea than a large one, and he did much to inspire other long-distance voyages. One of the most ambitious must be that of two Breton brothers, Henri and Raymond Rallier du Baty, who in 1908 bought a 45-ton ketch and, with four professional fishermen as crew, sailed to the Kerguelen Islands in the Roaring Forties midway between Africa and Australia. The two brothers spent a year on the islands, earning their living by killing seals and selling the oil, and then continued to New Zealand, where they paid off the crew, sold their boat, and returned home.

In conventional yachting, Dixon Kemp's rating system not only boosted the development of small craft, a few extremely large yachts were built to his rule as well, perhaps the best known being the *Britannia*, which belonged to the Prince of Wales

Hauling in a jib aboard *Columbia* during training for her successful defence of the America's Cup in 1899.

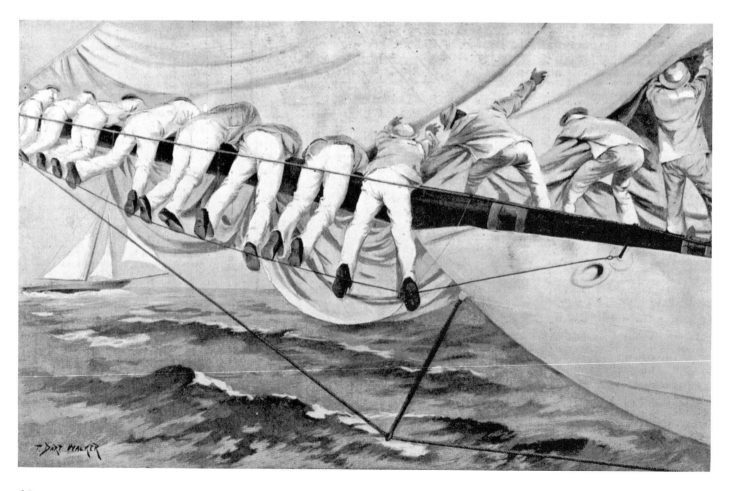

Manoeuvring before the start of the
1899 America's Cup series.

Sir Thomas Lipton, the man who kept
the America's Cup alive for over thirty
years, aboard *Erin* in 1915.

(later Edward VII) (see pp.70–1). She was one of four large British yachts produced in 1893, the others being *Calluna*, *Satanita*, and the Earl of Dunraven's America's Cup challenger, *Valkyrie II*. The Americans built no less than five new boats, *Vigilant*, *Pilgrim*, *Jubilee*, *Colonia* and *Navahoe*, from which they chose *Vigilant*, designed by Nathaniel Herreshoff, to be their defender in the Cup series that year. When the first race of the series was called off through lack of wind, *Valkyrie II* had a lead of twenty-five minutes, which led to a furore in the American press – no one had ever held such a lead against the defenders. However, the series was eventually won by *Vigilant*, and so the Cup stayed in New York.

Dunraven sailed to New York again two years later in 1895 to challenge for the Cup with a new boat, *Valkyrie III*. Unfortunately this challenge was to be bedevilled by arguments once more. Dunraven thought he saw the American yacht, *Defender*, adding 13 tons of ballast the night before the first race, and he put in a complaint. The Americans, meanwhile, were hardly pleased by a collision at the beginning of the second race, in which *Valkyrie III* was clearly at fault. She continued to race, and won by just over two minutes. In the third race, Dunraven crossed the start line, but on seeing the course was not clear promptly sailed back and dropped his racing flag, while the American yacht sailed on and took the race and the Cup. Dunraven felt he had not been given a fair chance in the series, and a long and acrimonious enquiry did not help matters, although it became obvious that the allegations concerning the added ballast were unfounded.

Perhaps if *Britannia* had crossed the Atlantic and made a challenge the Cup would have been won, but the Prince of Wales, as heir to the throne, confined his racing to waters closer to home. Other members of the Prince's family were equally fond of the sport, and his son, the Duke of York, later King George V, commissioned a one-rater, the *White Rose*, in the 1890s, and entered her in class races. It is recorded that he ordered the boat on a Monday, and four and a half days later she was launched and had won her first race, an example of speedy yacht-building that it is difficult to imagine today.

Britannia

Royal party aboard *Britannia* in 1920.

In the early 1920s *Britannia* was gaff-rigged, but the Jackyard topsail has disappeared.

Giles, King Edward VII's regular pilot, as drawn by Lord Albemarle.

Britannia was one of Britain's most celebrated yachts. She was built in 1893 for Edward, Prince of Wales, at Partick on the Clyde by D. & W. Henderson to the plans of G.L. Watson.

Constructed of wood on steel frames to Dixon Kemp's Length and Sail Area Rule, she was $121\frac{1}{2}$ feet (37 m) long overall, 88 feet (26.8 m) at the waterline, displaced 159 tons, spread 10,327 square feet (960 sq m) of canvas, and started her career as a 151-rater. She thrashed the American yacht *Navahoe* in twelve out of thirteen races in 1893, and the following year raced against and beat the winning America's Cup defender *Vigilant*. Despite the royal owner, competitors such as *Valkyrie II* gave no quarter when racing, and after one spectacular collision in 1893 between the two boats, *Valkyrie's* crew cut away *Britannia's* bowsprit in order to extricate themselves. On another occasion a member of *Britannia's* crew, whilst hoisting the mainsail, fell upon the prince and knocked him unconscious!

On the introduction of time handicaps, which allowed small boats to compete with larger ones, the Prince became bored with big boat racing, and he sold *Britannia* in 1897. However four years later, as King Edward VII, he repurchased her, and after cruising for a year, he returned to racing again.

After World War I, King George V had *Britannia* refitted for racing. Out went the typical jackyard cutter rig with reefing topmast, to be replaced by the Marconi rig and fixed topmast, but she retained the gaff mainsail and long luffed topsail. In 1931 she was given a full Bermudan rig, with a mast height of 165 feet (50.3 m) and setting 8,700 square feet (809 sq m) of sail. In 1935 Charles Nicholson redesigned the rig with a reduced mast height of $156\frac{1}{2}$ feet (47.6 m) and a sail area of 8,337 square feet (775 sq m). Throughout all these changes, she remained a brilliant racer. In all she participated in 635 races, winning 231 first prizes.

Her regular racing schedule was not restricted to British waters, and for some seasons she spent the early months of the year competing on the French Riviera. Her end came in 1936 after the death of George V, when under the terms of his will she was taken out to sea and scuttled off the Isle of Wight.

George V was known as the sailor king, and loved getting to sea in his yacht.

Lord Brassey's Sunbeam

The *Sunbeam* was a renowned and beautiful steam auxiliary yacht built in the mid-eighteenth century. She measured 531 tons, and, rigged as a three-masted topsail schooner, set 8,333 square feet (770 sq m) of sail. She also had an auxiliary 350 horsepower engine and a feathering propeller. Her 37,000-mile cruise around the world in 1876-7 was the subject of one of the Victorian age's best-selling travel books, *The Voyage of the 'Sunbeam'*, written by Lady Brassey, wife of the owner, who accompanied her husband on the voyage.

Lady Brassey was an enthusiastic sailor and a fine and articulate observer. The voyage had its share of discomfort, as was only to be expected in a ship the size of a medium trading vessel of the time, but generally the family and friends lived on board in considerable style, in accommodation that would seem luxurious today. *Sunbeam* was beautifully fitted out, and was maintained and operated in a way that put warships to shame. Her arrival in the United States created a sensation, as although large auxiliary powered yachts existed, none were built or managed to quite the same standard.

Lady Brassey was eventually buried at sea from her beloved yacht in 1887. Lord Brassey continued to make long-distance cruises, and in 1905 *Sunbeam* participated in a race for the Kaiser's Gold Cup from New York to the Needles, but she had the indignity of having her propeller removed for the race. This was just one of perhaps ten Atlantic crossings made by the yacht.

Sunbeam saw service as an auxiliary during World War I, and was bought afterwards by Lord Runciman. She was finally broken up in 1929.

Lord Brassey at the wheel.

Lord and Lady Brassey (seated) with some of their guests aboard *Sunbeam* in the Malacca Straits, 1874.

The *Sunbeam* under sail in 1905. Although she had an engine, she used sail whenever possible in her world voyage.

The main saloon. It had most of the creature comforts of a large house.

MONTE BRE LUGANO

SPERANZA HOTEL DU LAC

STRESA
LAC MAJEUR

OPULENCIA

VICTORIA HOTEL

ALICANTE

RHUM

NAROLIA

40 % vol

100 c

COTISATION SECURITÉ SOCIALE

G&P

N° 102 Déposé

Ets ARNAUD 15 rue Abel Laurent 75012 PARIS

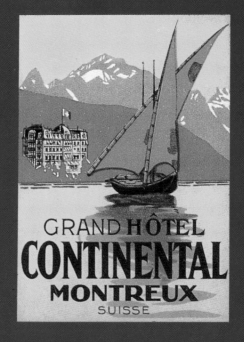

GRAND HÔTEL
CONTINENTAL
MONTREUX
SUISSE

GRANDE ALBERGO VITTORIA

NERVI

COLUMBUS HOTEL · ROMA ·

The British royal family was not alone amongst royalty in its love of yachting. Kaiser Wilhelm II of Germany had his *Meteor*, which raced at Cowes, using British crews until 1907 when national pride forced him to replace them with Germans. In 1905 the Kaiser presented a cup for a transatlantic race from Sandy Hook, just outside New York Harbour, to the Needles off the Isle of Wight. The race attracted eleven entries, ranging from 180 to 1,300 tons, and including square-rigged auxiliary yachts such as Lord Brassey's *Sunbeam* (see pp.72–3). It was won by a three-masted schooner *Atlantic*, skippered by the renowned Scotsman Charlie Barr, in a voyage of twelve days, four hours and one minute – a record that was to stand for more than seventy years. It is said that when the owner complained that Captain Barr was overpressing the boat, the captain locked him into his cabin for two days! All but one of the boats finished within fifteen days.

There was no love lost between the royal relatives of England and Germany, and there is a story that on one occasion when asked the Prince of Wales's whereabouts, the Kaiser replied that his cousin was sailing with his grocer, a reference to Sir Thomas Lipton. The Prince is rumoured to have shown his feelings about this remark by kicking a silver cup he had just won, which had been presented by the Kaiser, off the side of his boat. Another royal supporter of British regattas was the King of Spain, whose Fife-designed 15-metre class *Hispania* was a regular entrant until World War I. Since racing was taken very seriously, and collisions were not uncommon, it is easy to imagine the international repercussions had there been a major accident. Fortunately nothing crucial occurred between the royal owners, but the danger was ever present, as was shown by a collision between *Valkyrie II* and *Satanita* in 1894 which led to the former sinking and one crewman being killed.

Owning a yacht became a matter of status amongst many heads of state, and most had imposing steam yachts which they used for state visits and for attending regattas, even if not all wanted to race their own sailing yachts. Many of these floating palaces were designed and built in Britain, which was then the world leader in ship construction. Perhaps the strangest yacht ever was the *Livadia*, built in Scotland in 1880 for Czar Alexander II of Russia. She was modelled on a round warship of 1875, the *Admiral Popov*, which the Czar had liked because it did not make him feel seasick. The *Livadia* had an almost circular hull beneath the water, with yacht-like upper works. She measured 3,900 tons, and had a length of 235 feet (71.68 m) and beam under water of 153 feet (46.67 m). Her three propellers gave her a speed of 17 knots, but she could also set sails on five masts. Despite her odd appearance, she was very comfortable and stayed in commission until 1926.

Previous page and above: A selection of hold labels, tourist stickers and cigar labels featuring yacht subjects, *c*.1905–50.

Carved tillers from the *Clytie* and the *Fiona* in the possession of the Royal Thames Yacht Club.

A typical dayboat of the early half of the twentieth century, painted by Daniel Sherrin.

Apart from royalty, there were still a few sportsmen who were prepared to spend a king's ransom on the very best boats, not least the man who was to dominate the America's Cup racing for the next thirty-two years, and who introduced a new aspect to this competition which is commonplace today, using it for business promotion – Sir Thomas Lipton. Lipton was a self-made millionaire, famous for his tea company, and he entered an unconditional challenge under the auspices of the Royal Ulster Yacht Club, leaving the New York Yacht Club to make the conditions. His boat, *Shamrock I,* was conceived as an out and out racer to the American rules and excluded all the comforts that were common on board, although we would probably consider her pretty luxurious today. To defend the Cup, an American millionaire, Pierpont Morgan, commissioned Herreshoff to design a new boat, *Columbia*. A prerequisite was that a challenger had to sail to America, but Lipton obtained permission to have *Shamrock* towed over, and she was hurriedly prepared for the first race, which was due to take place on 3 October 1899.

The Americans had learned some lessons from the Dunraven affair in 1895, and this time an Act of Congress allowed the Coastguard and Navy to clear the course of spectators. Unfortunately, the wind was light for the first two weeks of the attempted racing, and no races were finished. Eventually, *Columbia* won all three races, and yet another challenge for the Cup had failed. However, the British had gained good experience, and the series was without dispute, which did much to restore friendly feelings between the two countries.

Lipton returned two years later in 1901 with *Shamrock II* and lost again to *Columbia*. The superiority of the Americans has been attributed to the skill of their skipper, Charlie Barr, who had also sailed in the previous series and skippered *Defender* in 1895.

In 1903 Lipton's third challenge, *Shamrock III*, contested and lost the America's Cup to *Reliance*. Designed by Herreshoff, *Reliance* was an outstanding yacht, the largest ever to defend the Cup. She was 144 feet (43.92 m) long overall, with a mast height of 196 feet (59.78 m) and a sail area of 16,000 square feet (1,488 sq m).

Transatlantic races were now regularly staged by American yachtsmen. They also introduced two new races in 1905 and 1906. These were the Trans-Pacific Race, over a distance of 2,225 miles (4,125 km) from Los Angeles to Honolulu, and a race of 600 miles (1,112 km) from Brooklyn to Bermuda. The latter was the brain-child of T.F. Day,

Shamrock II dismasted during training for the 1901 America's Cup. 110 feet of mast and 14,000 square feet of sail crashed overside, but no one aboard, including King Edward VII, was hurt.

Opposite: A study of raw power as *Shamrock* races in 1912.

Below, left: *Columbia* beating *Shamrock II* in the first race of the 1901 America's Cup series.

The Americans were not convinced that Sir Thomas Lipton would succeed in his efforts to win the America's Cup, as this cartoon from the *New York Tribune* shows.

IT'S NAILED FAST!
Sir Thomas—I've come to lift the Cup.

editor of *Rudder* magazine and a keen exponent of the safety and seaworthiness of small yachts. It became known as the Bermuda Race, and was re-established in 1923 as a regular event.

In the first decade of the twentieth century rules for the rating of yachts were a source of some controversy, as thirteen European nations had agreed to an International Rule which defined boats according to a formula represented by metres, whereas America had opted for the Universal Rule, which defined each of the different classes by a letter of the alphabet. Both rules were an attempt to provide a rating formula so that boats of differing design could be built yet where the sum of certain factors, such as length, sail area, keel depth, etc., added up to a measurement which could be used for handicapping in relation to other boats. Unfortunately the parameters employed by the two rules differed, so a yacht built in Europe to the International Rule might be at a disadvantage if she were to be measured for the American Universal Rule.

Sir Thomas Lipton challenged for the America's Cup again in 1907 after these rules had been finalized, but he specified that he wanted to race under the American Universal Rule. The members of the New York Yacht Club, however, saw no reason why they should not select whatever craft they liked as the defender, regardless of the rules. Lipton not unnaturally withdrew his challenge, but he approached the New York Yacht Club

The launch of *Shamrock IV* from Campers and Nicholson in 1912 with *HMS Victory* in the background.

BOSTON INSURANCE COMPANY

BOSTON
MASSACHUSETTS

———

CAPITAL
$1,000,000

SURPLUS
$2,000,000

FIRE, MARINE, YACHT, AUTOMOBILE
—AND—
TOURISTS' BAGGAGE
INSURANCE

———

The commercial aspect of the America's Cup: the cover of a blotting pad showing *Resolute* and *Vanitie*.

again in 1912. However, the club had not changed its attitude, and, perhaps exasperated, he finally entered an unconditional challenge in 1913, which was accepted. Charles E. Nicholson designed *Shamrock IV* for Lipton, and Nathaniel Herreshoff designed *Resolute* for Cornelius Vanderbilt, but World War I broke out when *Shamrock IV* was halfway across the Atlantic, and the series was postponed.

The early 1900s had beeen halcyon days for yachting. Many new small classes appeared as people sought to find a boat that could race on level terms and that was suited to local conditions. The factors that decide whether or not a class of dinghy will be successful are the suitability of the initial design, its ability to attract the yachting public, and the cost. Two classes designed at this time illustrate these principles and continue to be sailed enthusiastically today. The X One design was created in 1909 by the British designer A. Westmacott as a small day sailer. Its popularity was limited to the waters of the Solent and Poole, but here it has retained solid support, and each year Cowes Regatta can count on sixty or seventy turning out for some hard-fought racing. In 1911 an American, William Gardner, designed a hard chine boat measuring 22 feet 9 inches (6.94 m), with fin and bulb keel, which was christened the *Star*. It was very successful, and although changes have been made over the years so that it is now built of glass reinforced plastic, it is basically the same as the original, and remains one of the Olympic classes.

As the war engulfed the world in 1914, yachts were laid up, and crews were siphoned off into military service. Although few people realized it, the period of the great fleets of enormous yachts was past. But in the previous hundred years the sport had developed from the preserve of a few into a popular pastime for many, and it was this broadened support which was to cause its revitalization when the war was over.

4
Yachting between the Wars

(1918–1939)

Yacht Rigs

The earliest Dutch yachts were single-masted, with a large gaff mainsail, staysail and jib. Later a square topsail was added. The large Stuart yachts were square-rigged on the mainmast, with a lateen mizzen (triangular aft-sail). As work boats were copied, their rigs were adopted as well. The square sails disappeared, and a lug topsail was set above the gaff mainsail. These rigs depended upon a heavy mast supported by hefty shrouds and stays. There was no fixed backstay, as the gaff prevented one being rigged, and the mast was usually raked so that the shrouds provided the aft support. Topmasts for square rigs were usually of weighty construction, but became lighter with the introduction of the lug topsail.

In America, the schooners were similarly rigged with large gaff mainsails and foresails and large jibs. The throat of the gaff was taken close to the masthead. The topmast on the mainmast rarely set a sail, but was often the preserve of the owner's houseflag. All the yachts of the early years carried bowsprits.

The first change to this basic form of rigging came in the nineteenth century, when the lug topsail began to be replaced by a triangular sail, the luff of which was attached to the topmast. By the 1850s both types of topsail were still employed, but the greater efficiency of a sail attached to the mast led to a decline in the lugsail.

Dinghies followed the larger yachts, but the gunter rig became popular in place of the lugsail because it provided a comparatively large sail area on a small mast.

The major change in rigs came at the beginning of the twentieth century with the Bermudan rig. By doing away with the heavy gaff, a lighter mast could be used, and this in turn led to longer masts that required additional support. The 'Marconi' rig was the solution, so named because of its resemblance to the aerial masts of the time. The support was provided by 'spreaders' in pairs athwart the mast, with shrouds running to both the inner end of the spreader, and via its outer end to the masthead, or, on a mast with more than one set of spreaders, to the inner end of the next set. The Bermudan rig also allowed the erection of permanent backstays, and this in turn enabled greater tension to be put on the forestay and created a flatter headsail. Masts also grew taller, and as a result became as heavy as the old shorter gaff masts. To reduce weight, masts were constructed hollow, but it was the arrival of aluminium that permitted even longer masts, because their light weight did not require an enormously heavy keel to balance them.

Aluminium remains the most popular mast material, but lighter materals are in use, such as carbon-fibre-reinforced plastic. The advent of a more technical approach to rigging has led to a wide variety of mast sections and multi-spreader rigs. At the extreme end are the 'wing masts', which resemble a very narrow aeroplane wing set vertically on a pivot on the boat's deck. These have the advantage of providing a much more efficient leading edge to the sail, and therefore give greater power. Their main drawback is that they cannot be 'reefed', and in strong winds they alone can sometimes provide more power than the boat can handle safely.

Bermudan Cutter

Gaff Cutter

Bermudan Schooner

Staysail Schooner

Gaff Schooner

Topsail Schooner

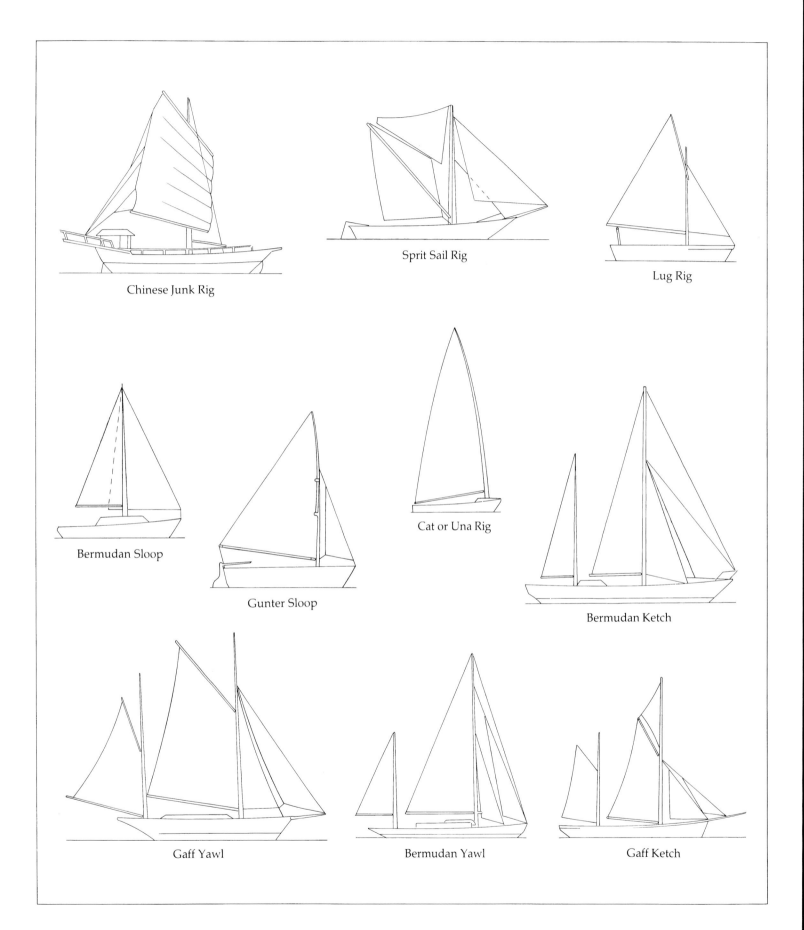

Chinese Junk Rig

Sprit Sail Rig

Lug Rig

Bermudan Sloop

Gunter Sloop

Cat or Una Rig

Bermudan Ketch

Gaff Yawl

Bermudan Yawl

Gaff Ketch

In 1921 America belatedly switched to the International Rule for yachts under 12 metres, and the North American Yacht Racing Union was formed. Henceforward Americans and Europeans were building and racing the same boats, and class racing, at least in the metre classes, became truly international. Almost at once a new cup was presented, the British America Cup, for an annual competition in 6-metre yachts between the two nations. The 6-metre class measured close to 40 feet (12.2 m) in overall length and had a waterline just short of 24 feet (7.32 m), although these parameters varied from design to design, as architects strove to produce a faster boat within the rules. British competitors had more experience of the class, and they won at Cowes in 1921, and again at Oyster Bay in the United States in 1922. A third win the following year gave them the cup outright. A new cup was presented in 1928, but by this time the American contestants had caught up, and they won outright with three straight series. The event continued, but was dominated by the Americans. Their supremacy was partly due to their analysing of race results and tank testing to improve hulls, but these techniques were copied, so that by 1932 there was little difference between Britain and America in this respect. In rigs and sail handling, however, American yachts had jumped ahead, and whereas the British were carrying a choice of only two headsails, the Americans had six and parachute spinnakers. A young American designer, Olin Stephens, had his first winning boat, the *Goose*, in this competition. She was the earliest of many outstanding craft in his long career.

Although proper ocean racing had made a start early in the century, and the Bermuda Race was revived in 1923, run by the newly formed Cruising Club of America, it was not until 1925 that there was a comparable race on a regular basis in European waters. Weston Martyr sailed in the 1923 and 1924 Bermuda Races and returned to England determined to instigate a similar event. The course he chose was almost exactly the same length as the Bermuda Race, 605 miles (1,122 km) long, starting from Cowes and proceeding along the English south coast and out to the Fastnet Rock off the south-west coast of Ireland, then back south of the Scilly Islands to Plymouth. The winner of the first race was George Martin in his converted Le Havre pilot cutter *Jolie Brise*. In fact the first Fastnet Race was more a cruise started together with the same destination than an ocean race in the usual sense. However, the contestants enjoyed themselves so much that they decided it should become an annual event, and they formed a new yacht club, the Ocean Racing Club, with George Martin as its first Commodore, for the management of this and other races. In 1931 the club became the Royal Ocean Racing Club, and had its headquarters in London. By 1939 the club held over thirty ocean races in a season, and their popularity did much to persuade other European nations to follow along these lines.

The Fastnet Race quickly became a classic. Part of its attraction lay in the increasing enthusiasm for crewed medium-distance racing, but it also provided more difficult conditions than the Bermuda Race, which has regular and predictable weather and where the only navigational problem is the north-east setting Gulf Stream. The English Channel, on the other hand, is a crowded shipping lane with considerable tides, and the weather is dominated by a succession of depressions and associated fronts which create widely varying wind directions and speeds. The ideal boat for this situation was considered to be the well-tried work boat type of fast cruiser, but in 1926 a new craft arrived on the scene. This was William Fife's design *Hallowe'en*, built for a Colonel Baxendale, and based on the International Rule 15-metre class. She won the race in the record time of three days, nineteen hours and five minutes, a time that is respectable by present day standards. Two years later in 1928 the Fastnet Race saw the debut of what might be called the first of the modern American offshore racers, the staysail schooner *Nina*, designed by Starling Burgess. She won the race with ease.

Above and below: Swiss hotel labels, c.1950 and c.1920.

The *Jolie Brise*, winner of the first
Fastnet Race, photographed in 1926.

The Fastnet became a biennial event in 1929, and the next race in 1931 was won by *Dorade*, a boat which was to establish many new features for ocean racers. Designed by Olin Stephens (see p.94), she had been victorious in a transatlantic race that year, and was to win the Fastnet again in 1933. *Dorade's* ascendancy was due as much to the lightness of her build as to her lines and the way she was sailed, but it took her victories to convince the yachting authorities on each side of the Atlantic that such a light boat could be simultaneously fast and seaworthy. The American successes, far from discouraging the British sailors, led to greater interest in the Fastnet Race, which had seventeen entrants in 1935, when it was won by yet another Stephens design, *Stormy Weather*. Only in 1939 did the British regain their own trophy, mainly because Americans were deterred from entering by the gathering war clouds in Europe. The race was won by *Bloodhound*, designed by Charles E. Nicholson. Apart from the war years, the Fastnet Race has been run on every odd year since, alternating with the Bermuda Race, and it attracts a large international fleet.

Dinghy sailing progressed and cultivated a strong international following. The best known of the British boats was the *International 14-footer* (4.27 m), designed by Frank Morgan-Giles. A national class was formed after World War I, and in 1927 it was given international status. In the same year the Prince of Wales, later King Edward VIII, presented a cup to the class which became known as the Prince of Wales Cup and was considered the Blue Riband for dinghies. Like many dinghy classes, the rules of the class were changed to incorporate new innovations. Bamboo masts had been allowed early on, and in 1928 the gunter rig was replaced by the Bermudan rig. During this year a British designer

Yacht Designers

One of the all-time greats of yacht design, Nathaniel Herreshoff.

Early yachts were usually designed and built by a Master Shipwright, who used his eye and experience to create a fine fast craft. The change to a more scientific approach came in the 1870s when Dixon Kemp in England and Nathaniel Herreshoff in the United States began developing designs. The former was one of the founders of the Yacht Racing Association, later the Royal Yachting Association, whilst the latter went on to experiment with catamarans and produce a number of highly successful America's Cup defenders, including *Vigilant* (1893), *Defender* (1895), *Columbia* (1899 and 1901), *Reliance* (1903) and *Resolute* (1920).

Edward Burgess of Boston, Massachusetts, had only a brief career as a designer from 1885 until his premature death in 1891, but during that time he had three victorious America's Cup defenders, *Puritan, Mayflower,* and *Volunteer.*

George Watson of Glasgow started designing in 1877, but achieved his first international winner with *Madge* in 1879. He subsequently designed *Thistle*, which was narrowly beaten for the America's Cup by *Volunteer*. His most famous design was *Britannia*, built for the Prince of Wales in 1893, but he also had other famous boats such as *Valkyrie II, Shamrock II,* and *Meteor,* the latter owned by Kaiser Wilhelm II of Germany. Watson's successor in Britain was undoubtedly Charles Nicholson, who also took up the mantle as designer for the America's Cup, producing *Shamrock IV* and *V* in 1914 and 1930, as well as the two *Endeavours* for 1934 and 1937.

The American leaders in design in the thirties, from left to right: Starling Burgess, Olin Stephens, Rod Stephens, and Drake Sparkman.

These early designers created the art of naval architecture. The profession flourished in the first half of this century, perhaps the most outstanding practitioners being the Stephens brothers, Olin and Roderick, and their company Sparkman and Stephens in the United States. Their initial large design was *Dorade*, considered light in 1931, but full of technical innovation and above all a winner. Like many yacht architects, they could turn their skills to other purposes, and they were also responsible for the DUKW amphibious vehicle used in World War II.

Naval architecture, specializing in yachts, has expanded since 1945. The modern designer uses computers as a matter of course to aid him, and technical practice has advanced well beyond the stage of tank testing. Although it may safely be described as a science today, art and natural flair still plays a part in producing a good-looking craft that manages to be just a little bit faster than her competitors.

Charles Nicholson, the leading British designer of the thirties.

Opposite: A silver model of the J Class *Candida.*

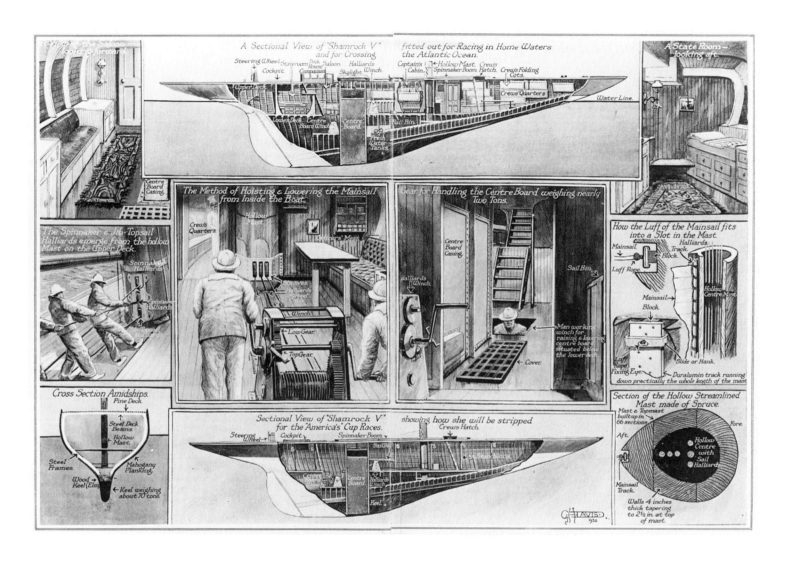

The *Illustrated London News* of May 1930 featuring *Shamrock V*.

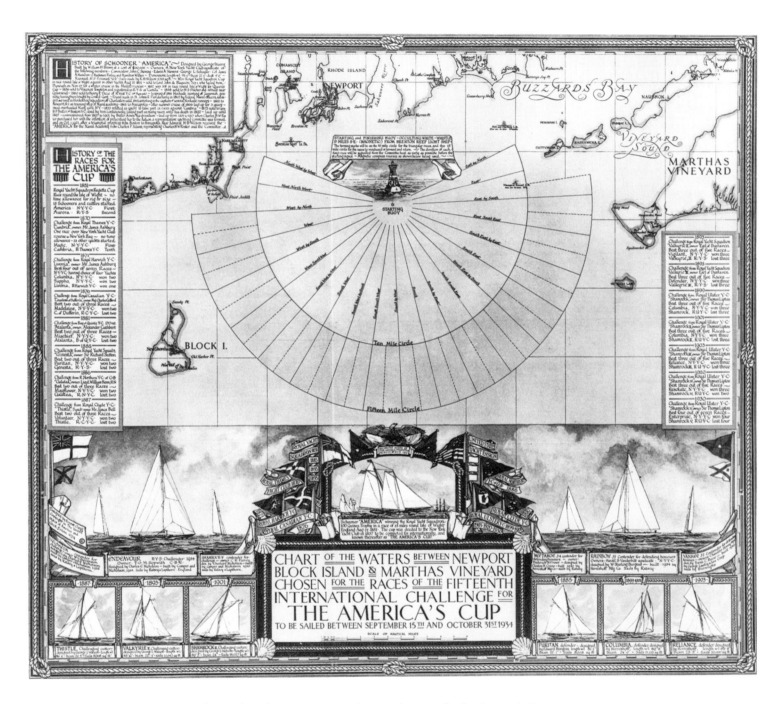

Decorative chart produced by the *Illustrated London News* in 1934, showing the arena for the America's Cup series.

Pouring the 90-ton lead keel of Sir Thomas Lipton's *Shamrock V* at the builder's yard, Camper and Nicholson . . .

. . . and laying her deck, in 1934.

The British challenge for the America's Cup in 1937. *Endeavour I* leading *Endeavour II*.

Above, right: *Ranger*, the successful defender of the America's Cup in 1937.

Havre in 1929. It was almost thirty years since Joshua Slocum had first circumnavigated the world alone, but if Gerbault was attempting to become the second man to achieve this, he failed, because Harry Pidgeon, a farmer's son from Iowa, had set sail in 1921 and returned to Los Angeles in 1925, pipping him to the post. Another to take the world route was the American, William A. Robinson, who sailed with a young Tahitian crew named Etera, in the 32-foot (9.76 m) *Svaap*.

Yachting was not immune to the effects of the Great Depression, which caused many owners to lay up their yachts, and others to postpone voyages. But as is so often the case in times of financial hardship, the wealthy appeared to suffer less than others. Even so, by the 1930s, when the cost of a large yacht was high even by today's standards, it took enormous wealth and considerable courage to think of building a large racing type, let alone of entering it for the America's Cup. However, although he was now eighty years old, Lipton wanted to make another attempt, and he commissioned *Shamrock V*, a J class yacht to the design of Charles Nicholson, for what was to be his final challenge. It appears that he waited until the race conditions were changed so that both the challenger and defender had to be built to Lloyds scantlings (the rules published by Lloyds which cover the strength of a hull and size of materials used in the construction), as he believed it unfair that the defender could be made more lightly than the challenger. The American eliminations were won by *Enterprise*, a remarkable boat, full of new technology, not least a duralium mast which was only two-thirds the weight of a hollow wooden one. The 1930 series was a whitewash, *Enterprise* proving the faster boat from the start and winning four straight races.

There were those such as King George V, who was Commodore of the Royal Yacht Squadron, and who doubted whether it was a good idea to make a further challenge, in view of the industrial conditions caused by the Great Depression. However, Sir Thomas Lipton had been planning a sixth challenge when he died in 1931, and after some discussion the mantle was taken up by the aircraft designer and builder T.O.M. Sopwith, who had already purchased *Shamrock V*. In 1931 the Europeans had adopted the American Universal Rule for yachts above 14.5 metres as measured by the International Rule. The J class of the Universal Rule seemed to be ideal for the challenge, which was issued by the Royal Yacht Squadron on Sopwith's behalf. A new boat, *Endeavour*, measuring 130 feet (39.65 m) overall and 83 feet (25.32 m) at the waterline, was designed and built by Charles Nicholson. She had good results in her outings in 1934 on the British circuit. Unfortunately, her paid crew decided to strike just before the yacht was due to sail to America and they had to be replaced by amateurs, who although of considerable experience, had no time to prepare. The American contestants chose a new boat named *Rainbow*, designed by Starling Burgess and owned by the railway millionaire W.S. Vanderbilt. The series was to be the best of seven races. Before the racing commenced the two crews were allowed to inspect each other's vessels, and the British noted that all the cabin fittings had been removed from *Rainbow*, thus making her lighter. A row ensued, which became known as the battle of the bathtubs; it was resolved when the Americans agreed that the British crew could remove *Endeavour's* cabin fittings — including the owner's bath!

The first race, on 15 September 1934, was abandoned due to lack of wind when *Rainbow* was ahead by about a mile (1.85 km). The second race, on the 17th, looked as if it might be a repeat of the first, with *Rainbow* taking the lead at the start. However, once Sopwith tacked for the mark, *Endeavour* pulled ahead and went on to win by two minutes and nine seconds. The third race, sailed in a fresh breeze, saw the two boats

Previous page: Rainbow and *Endeavour* in the final race of the 1934 America's Cup series, by John Steven Dews.

Mr and Mrs T.O.M. Sopwith steering *Endeavour* in 1934.

The era of the giant yachts. A J Class race in the 1930s.

locked together, *Endeavour* just in the lead for eight miles (14.83 km), and in spite of tearing her Genoa jib, winning by fifty-one seconds. *Endeavour* led in the fourth race and was six minutes ahead when the wind went light. Vanderbilt handed over the helm of *Rainbow* to Sherman Hoyt, who knew Sopwith from sailing against him in the Solent, and was aware that he always covered an opponent. Hoyt luffed up close to the wind and Sopwith followed, covering him until the point came when Hoyt knew he could head away from the wind to make the line. In the calm reaching conditions *Rainbow* was the better boat and clawed back a race. The rest of the series then went the Americans' way, but not without a fight: Hoyt only narrowly won another of the races by bluffing Sopwith on the final leg to the finish.

Only one thing marred the series, a dispute in the fourth race as to whether Sopwith had displayed his protest flag at *Rainbow's* failure to luff after a mark, as required by the racing rules. Sopwith hoisted it according to the British rules, and in agreement with the American observer carried on board, but the race committee ruled that it had to be shown at the time of the incident, not as the yacht approached the committee vessel. It left a deep scar in the British camp.

Nevertheless, Nicholson had produced a very fast boat, and, thus encouraged, Sopwith challenged again in 1937 with a new J boat, *Endeavour II*. In America, Starling Burgess teamed up with Olin Stephens to produce a radical new boat, *Ranger*, which was extensively tank tested before her design was finalized. She was decisively faster than any other American J class, and although Sopwith took both *Endeavours* across the Atlantic to hold his own trials and train his crew in the racing conditions, *Endeavour II* was easily beaten in four straight races.

This was the end of the J class. The yachts had become too expensive to build and campaign. The demise of these beautiful boats took much of the glamour out of racing and reduced the competition. Owners switched to the 12-metre class instead, and the 1939 season saw some exciting sailing when an American 12-metre, *Vim*, came across to Britain for the season and won nineteen of her twenty-seven starts. It is possible that a challenge for the America's Cup in this class might have followed shortly, but war intervened.

5
A Sport for All
(1945–1960)

Only one sailing event of note occurred between 1939 and 1945, and that was a single-handed circumnavigation by an Argentinian, Vito Dumas, in a 32-footer (9.76 m), *Legh II*. He departed from his homeland on 26 June 1942, and returned to Mar del Plata the following July, having stopped at Cape Town, Wellington in New Zealand, and Valparaiso in Chile. Although Dumas may have made a 'short' circumnavigation, in that he never came north of the Equator and so the distance he covered was considerably less than someone who sets out and returns to a port in the northern hemisphere, he can claim the credit of being the first to have made a circumnavigation within the southern hemisphere and south of Africa, Tasmania and Cape Horn.

Yachting took some time to recover from the war, and increased taxes and heavier costs meant that even syndicates could no longer afford to commission the giants of the pre-war years. The J class, the cream of yachting, had had its day, and the emphasis within the sport now transferred to ocean racers. The difference between the two lay not just in the size of boat, but in the type of racing. The Js were day sailers essentially – their races started and finished the same day, usually in fairly sheltered waters such as the Solent. The ocean racers were designed to go offshore and race overnight or, in some of the longer races, for a week or more. These yachts, a compromise between the out and out day racer and the cruiser, were fast, lightweight and seaworthy.

One of the earliest post-war ocean-racing yachts built in England was John Illingworth's *Myth of Malham*, designed by Laurent Giles. She was a 38-foot (11.59 m) cutter of light displacement, with fin keel and short overhangs. Illingworth also introduced masthead jibs on this boat, where the sail was hoisted right to the head of the

Previous page: The saloon on *Nirvana*. Originally built as a racer in 1950, she was subsequently bought by Nelson Rockefeller for private use.

The *6-metre* class *Llanoria* at Cowes in 1949, sailed by E. Mosbacher.

Dragon class racing at Cowes in 1949.
Blue Skies, Danae II, and *Typhon.*

mast instead of three-quarters or less of the way up as had been the custom. This feature was soon adopted generally. Although *Myth of Malham* proved highly successful, winning the Fastnet Race in 1947 and 1949, and winning her class until 1957, her lines were not universally admired, and she was described by the American magazine *Yachting* as a 'dreadful looking monstrosity'. However, she is now recognized as one of the milestones in ocean-racing design. Apart from the influence of her design and rig, she demonstrated how dramatically yacht sizes had been reduced, and another fifteen years passed before boats significantly larger than *Myth of Malham* became the norm again.

Illingworth was not only responsible for developments in yachts. Whilst serving in the Royal Navy in Australia at the end of the war, he was involved in establishing another great yachting event, the Sydney to Hobart Race. Organized by the Royal Yacht Club of Tasmania, and at 690 miles (1,280 km) slightly longer than the Bermuda and Fastnet Races, it is now recognized as a classic and forms part of the Southern Cross series. Although the course seems comparatively simple, the weather conditions on the edge of the Southern Ocean can provide a severe test for boats and crews.

Whilst offshore racing slowly recovered, an upsurge came about in dinghy racing, mainly due to the advent of better quality plywoods and new wood glues which had been developed for aircraft manufacture during the war. This enabled even unskilled people to build boats at home. One of the earliest of this type in Britain was the car-top dinghy subsequently christened the *Heron,* which was of lightweight hard chine plywood

W. H. Walker, *Fullers Clam Broth*, poster.

construction. A few years later a small dinghy, the *Mirror*, also designed for home construction, made its debut, and more than 50,000 were sold. Large fleets of dinghies were sailed not only on bays, rivers and estuaries, but in gravel ponds and reservoirs where there was room to lay out a simple course. Other wartime developments took longer to penetrate the sport, such as Dacron (Terylene) for sails and rope, nylon for spinnakers, and, in the 1960s, glass reinforced plastic for hull construction.

The advantage of glass reinforced plastic (GRP) construction lay in the fact that skilled shipwrights were not essential; it depended instead upon a highly polished mould onto which numerous layers of glass cloth were stuck together with resin in order to create each hull. The process was therefore cheap in comparison to the more traditional boat-building methods, and it also provided identical hulls. Small racing dinghies were the first to benefit from this system, but it soon spread to larger classes, and its lower costs enabled many more people to become boat owners. The process does require that the mould, taken off a full size plug, should be very accurate, since it is only the quality of the mould that restricts the output of hulls.

The first post-war Olympics took place in England, and sailing was very much involved. The *Dragon, Star, Swallow, Firefly,* and *6-metre* were used; the United States won two gold medals, and Britain, Denmark and Norway one each. In 1952 the Olympics were held at Helsinki in Finland, and the *Firefly* and *Swallow* were replaced by the *5.5 metre* and the *Finn* dinghy. The *Finn* is a single-handed dinghy which came in as a result of the rule that a host nation may introduce a new sport to the games. It has been an Olympic boat ever since, and is one that provides absolutely fair sailing, as the host nation supplies the boats for the competition, with each entrant drawing his particular boat in a ballot. By the Melbourne Olympics of 1956, the *6-metre* had been dropped, and the *Sharpie* introduced. In 1960 at Rome, the *Sharpie* gave way to the *Flying Dutchman* two-man dinghy designed by Van Essen, one of the most lively dinghies then available. By this time the trapeze was standard equipment on nearly all competitive racing dinghies. This allows the crew to clip onto a special wire attached high up the mast, and then place his feet on the gunwale so that his whole body weight is outside the boat to

Henri Gray, *Esterel-Plage*, poster.

110

Women in Yachting

'A girl who knows the ropes'. Women were no strangers to yachting in the 1860s, as this illustration shows.

Ladies' races, in which the yacht was helmed, if not crewed, by a woman, became popular in the 1890s and were a regular fixture by 1920.

The all-girl crew of *Maiden Great Britain* who participated in the 1989 Whitbread Round the World Race.

There is an old sailor's superstition that the sea grows angry at the sight of a woman, and for many years they were discouraged from going to sea for this reason. And even when ladies did start to join their husbands to attend regattas, it was as passengers, as the hard labour and rough conditions were considered to be unsuitable for those who were largely educated for more gentle pursuits. Despite this attitude, races solely for ladies were introduced towards the end of the nineteenth century, but they were the exception rather than the rule.

Women became more involved after World War I, and they began to crew regularly with family and friends, but even in the period immediately after World War II they were rarely found crewing on racing yachts. Small dinghies provided the real breakthrough. These required less physical strength, and women were quickly able to prove their abilities and that they could also be aggressive and competent skippers. The skills learned in dinghies were then transferred to larger boats.

Shortly after the war, Ann Davidson's solo voyage across the Atlantic showed that a lady could handle a boat alone and complete a hazardous journey as successfully as the men. There followed a number of long voyages by husband and wife teams, Edmund and Anne Pye, and Susan and Eric Hiscock. In 1971 Nicolette Milnes-Walker achieved the first non-stop east-west crossing of the Atlantic by a woman, and Claire Francis's much publicized participation in the 1972 OSTAR gave women's sailing a further boost.

The trend towards increasing female participation in yachting continues, and many women are no longer prepared to accept the role of cook and hostess. In 1988, the Olympics had a class for women for the first time, sailing in *470* dinghies. The separate class for women became necessary because their lighter weight puts them at a disadvantage, particularly in strong winds, when competing against men in dinghies.

Nowadays, as shown by Australian Kate Cottee who sailed non-stop around the world, and Florence Arthaud of France who has coped very effectively in sponsored multihull races, the ladies, although still outnumbered, are prepared to compete on equal terms, and in 1989 the Whitbread Round the World Race had an all-girl crewed entry for the first time.

MAIDEN GREAT BRITAIN

Yachting with the
ladies in the
Mediterranean in
1848.

This painting is
thought by some to
be of Sheila, Duchess
of Westminster, who
won an Olympic
bronze medal in her
8-metre *Saskia*. Her
navigator may be
Philip Hunloke, who
raced *Britannia*.

windward. The boat's stability is therefore greater and it may be driven much harder to windward, although this calls for considerable agility and fitness on the part of the crew.

Whilst there were many throughout the world who were taking up yacht racing for their weekends and holidays, there were also many who took up cruising. No one did more to emphasize the potential of small yachts in this field and spurred others to emulate them than Eric and Susan Hiscock, who, after an exploratory voyage to the Azores in their 24-foot (7.32 m) cutter *Wanderer II*, had a 30-foot (9.15 m) sloop built called *Wanderer III*, and set off in 1952 on a circumnavigation that was to last three years. Their book *Around the World in Wanderer III* has probably done more for seamanlike small boat sailing than anything else in the history of cruising, and is widely read, especially by those contemplating a long voyage.

In 1957 a new trophy, the Admiral's Cup, was presented by Sir Myles Wyatt, then the Admiral of the Royal Ocean Racing Club in London, for an international ocean-racing team contest. Initially the Admiral's Cup series incorporated races already established and run by the Royal Ocean Racing Club around the English coast: the Channel Race of about 200 miles (370 km); two inshore races of thirty miles (55.6 km) each, so named because they were set close to the coast; and the Fastnet Race. Any nation might enter, with a national team consisting of three boats. The competition was judged on a points basis, the winner gaining the number of points equal to the number of entries, with the last boat receiving just one point, but the Channel Race was worth double points and the Fastnet worth treble. The Admiral's Cup was the prototype for the similar Southern Cross series in Australia and the Southern Ocean Racing Conference series in America, and it has become one of the premier offshore racing competitions.

Racing for the 'Auld Mug', as Sir Thomas Lipton had called the America's Cup, took a long time to resume. No one thought that the J class should be resurrected, simply because these large boats would be too expensive, and it was suggested that a more practical boat might be considered. Captain John Illingworth proposed a large ocean-racer type which would have another career after the Cup races, as one of the problems with a specialized boat was that if defeated she could become a white elephant. However, the general feeling prevailed that the Cup boats should be somewhat distinctive, though on a smaller scale than the J class. Ultimately the waterline length for boats was reduced from 63 to 44 feet (19.22 to 13.42 m), and the 12-metre class was chosen for future America's Cup races. Although the 'Twelves' were large, rather specialized day boats, they were considerably smaller and therefore less costly than the Js, and they had the added advantage that they were already an internationally accepted class. These changes had to be approved by the Supreme Court of New York, which is the ultimate court of appeal for the America's Cup, since the original deed of gift was written in New York State. By 1957 all these details had been resolved and the first post-war challenge was issued by the Royal Yacht Squadron for a series to take place the following year.

In Britain one new boat, *Sceptre*, was commissioned, whilst the Americans built three, *Columbia*, *Weatherly* and *Easterner*. After lengthy trials, which did much to sharpen the American sailors, Olin Stephens's design, *Columbia*, was chosen to defend. The series itself was a very one-sided affair. The American boat proved decisively superior, and won four straight races in a competition that was remarkable for its good sportsmanship. The importance of the series did not lie so much in the result, however, as in the resurgence of interest in the Cup, which, 107 years since the first race, appeared to be eternally in the Americans' grasp.

In 1957, the year of the first Admiral's Cup, there was a less publicized affair which was to have far-reaching consequences as far as long-distance sailing was concerned,

Previous page: St. Tropez Marina, South of France.

A great designer, builder and sailor, Uffa Fox at the helm in 1955.

HRH the Duke of Edinburgh with Uffa Fox, sailing *Cowslip* at Cowes in 1968.

and particularly for single-handers. An American, Peter Tangvald, laid a bet of one dollar against an Englishman, Edward Allcard, that he could beat him in a single-handed race from Las Palmas in the Canary Islands to Antigua in the Caribbean. Tangvald won by two days. This was the first single-handed transatlantic race this century. Three years later it was followed by a longer one, from Plymouth in England to New York, which laid the foundations for the OSTAR (*Observer* Single-Handed Transatlantic Race): in 1960, 'Blondie' Hasler, a retired Royal Marine colonel, accepted a bet for half-a-crown (12½p) with Francis Chichester, for a single-handed race to New York. They were joined by three other yachts, manned by David Lewis, Jean Lacombe and Val Howells, and they persuaded the Royal Western Yacht Club to supervise the proceedings. All the contestants crossed safely, with Chichester winning in forty days. The race was such a success that the *Observer* newspaper offered to sponsor it in future at four-yearly intervals. This race propelled the event, and single-handed sailing across the Atlantic, from being considered within the realm of adventure sailing, into orthodox racing. The subject became front-page news for the next decade, during which all the possible major single-handed voyages were achieved.

6
Modern Times
(1960–1990s)

By 1960 the world had overcome the effects of the previous war, and there was sufficient prosperity to encourage yachting to sustain its expansion, which has lasted right through to the 1990s. The 1960s saw ocean racing become more international, more challenges for the America's Cup than in any equivalent period in its history, dinghy building and sailing become a hobby for everyman, and single- and short-handed racing emerge from being a pastime for a small fringe.

In thirty years, yachting has become more specialized. There are now innumerable series to choose from, encompassing so many different branches of the sport that it would be impossible for one person to attend them all, even though air travel has made this easier. The broadening of the sport is such that it can no longer be considered seriously in general terms; the major specializations need separate treatment.

Previous page: 12-metre yachts close racing on a spinnaker run.

Dinghies and Windsurfing

Glass reinforced plastics (GRP) have largely replaced wood as the basic building material for the modern dinghy. Perhaps the most successful dinghy worldwide has been the single-handed *Laser* designed by Bruce Kirby, in which the hull and deck are bonded together, enclosing a large volume of air to provide buoyancy even when the boat has been capsized. It has a simple unsupported mast which breaks down into two lengths to facilitate car-top or trailer transportation. Over 100,000 of these boats have been built in factories around the world.

Smaller dinghies for training have also been introduced, designed with safety in mind to enable children as young as six years old to learn to sail. The *Optimist* class has been the most broadly used internationally, and may be seen racing in sheltered waters all over Europe.

The façade and shop interior of Captain O. M. Watts Ltd., the ultimate yachting chandler's, which has been in Piccadilly since 1926.

The fastest of the Olympic yachts, the two-man *Tornado* catamaran.

Surfing has long been a popular activity, particularly in and around the Pacific Ocean, where surfers can lie or stand on their surfboards as they rush towards the beach on the face of a large breaking wave. In the 1960s a mast with a sail was attached to one of these boards, and a new sailing sport was born. Windsurfing, as it is called, has gained a huge following in a very short space of time, partly because of the low cost of the equipment, but also because it is easy to master and yet can provide very fast and exciting sailing. The world record for the highest average speed under sail over a distance of 500 metres is held by windsurfer Eric Beale of Great Britain, who was timed at an average speed of $40\frac{1}{2}$ knots at Les Saintes Maries de la Mer in France in November 1988. This event grew from an annual series held at Portland in Dorset in which any vessel can be entered and timed. At first the purpose of this competition was to ascertain the optimum speeds of dinghies such as the *Flying Dutchman*, but it soon attracted people who were solely interested in creating a vessel that could outsail everything over the distance.

Ocean Racing

The Duke of Edinburgh is said to have compared yachting with standing beneath a cold shower tearing up £5 notes. A crewman on an ocean racer beating into a heavy sea commented, as water descended on him through an open hatch, that this remark applied to owners: for the rest it was like being revolved in a cold washing machine! Ocean racing is a tough and frequently uncomfortable experience. Although there are as many sunny, calm days as there are rough, wet ones, it is the challenge of competing regardless of the varying sea conditions that makes the sport so exhilarating. The skipper may be able to afford the yacht, but its performance is dependent upon the teamwork of the whole crew.

The Olympic single-handed *Finn* dinghy class racing at Kiel.

Sailboards competing in the Aloah Classic, 1988.

Opposite: The thrill of yachting at a price most can afford.

Such numbers of people were taking to the sport of yachting by the 1960s that the racing calendar had to be enlarged to accommodate the many new competitors. The Admiral's Cup series had five competing nations in 1957 and 1959, by 1965 this was up to eight, and by the 1970s there were no less than eighteen nations. Some idea of the raised standards can be realized from the number of boats competing for selection for their national teams. In Britain in 1963 there were six, and ten years later there were thirty-two. This series has now been extended to include two extra inshore races, so the boats now have to sail a total of four 30 or 40 mile (55/74 km) races, in addition to the Channel Race and the Fastnet Race. In Australia the Southern Cross circuit and in the United States the Florida-based Southern Ocean Racing Conference have shown a corresponding growth. New series based upon the same formula, such as the Kenwood Cup in Hawaii, are being added to the international racing programme.

What seemed to be a great advance occurred in 1970 when two rating systems, the Cruising Club of America (CCA) and the Royal Ocean Racing Club (RORC), were replaced by one, the International Offshore Rule (IOR). All existing boats were remeasured to this formula thus allowing owners from all over the world to race each other under a common handicap system. Unfortunately the IOR encouraged lightweight boats, which, because of the weight-saving in their construction, do not have a long lifespan. There has been a move away from the IOR as owners have decided that they would rather build stronger boats and race to a simpler formula. In 1984 Britain and France introduced the Channel Handicap System, but more recently the American International Measurement System is coming into favour.

The start of the celebrated Fastnet Race.

Although many offshore races such as the Channel Race are limited to a weekend, there has also been a development of individual but longer races such as the Middle Sea Race first run by the Royal Malta Yacht Club in 1967. This race is around Malta, Lampedusa and Sicily, a distance of 607 miles (1,125 km). In 1971 the South African Cruising Association organized an ocean race from Cape Town to Rio de Janeiro in Brazil, a distance of about 3,500 miles (6,489 km). Except for one yacht which struck a whale, all the boats reached Rio in time for the famous carnival, which, according to the competitors, was a greater danger than the race itself! This race has been repeated several times, but politics have forced the destination to be changed to Uruguay, as Brazil will no longer participate in events starting in South Africa. More recently the Royal Hong Kong Yacht Club has introduced the China Sea Race from Hong Kong to Manila in even years, and a race to San Fernando, also in the Philippines, in odd years. All of these races are very much international affairs, sometimes requiring teams of yachts and crews to be ferried to venues at considerable cost.

Gradually yachts grew bigger, a minority reaching the upper limit of the IOR, a 70-foot (21.4 m) rating, which could mean a boat of 80 feet (24.1 m) in length and requiring a crew of up to twenty sailors. These boats, known as Maxis, eventually started their own series, but because of their cost, ownership was restricted to syndicates, wealthy individuals, or sponsors. Fortunately, people who have less time or smaller budgets for racing are catered for in the numerous series of local offshore races in most of the yachting countries of the world. One such series in Britain, the Junior Offshore Group, was formed to race boats below the then RORC rule limit, specifically to provide offshore racing at less expense in smaller boats.

For those who prefer the kind of racing where the first boat over the finish line is the winner, yachts reminiscent of the 1890 Raters have been introduced, which adopt the old title of tons to describe their size and rating. These boats are built to a fixed rating but vary considerably in design. A one-tonner is the equivalent of 30.55 feet of rating under the IOR; $\frac{3}{4}$-tonners measure 24.55 feet; $\frac{1}{2}$-tonners 22.05 feet; and $\frac{1}{4}$-tonners 18.55 feet. The $\frac{1}{4}$-ton class was intended to be a bridge for dinghy sailors to join the offshore racing fraternity, being little more than large dinghies with the minimum of accommodation below deck. However, as designers elaborated on the theme, and the costs escalated, the even smaller mini-tonner has been instituted, which rates at 16.55 feet, in yet another attempt to keep sailing within the reach of less affluent yachtsmen.

However good the handicap system, designers will sooner or later find a loophole that gives their boats an edge, and the rule is usually modified to prevent boats becoming too extreme. These modifications generally work to the detriment of older boats despite the introduction of an age allowance. They also increase the costs of measurement, and in recent years have promoted ultra-light and, some would say, unseaworthy yachts. A major snag in lightweight construction has been that many ocean racers are no longer suitable for conversion to a new life as cruisers at the end of their careers. Since this affects the resale value, the overall effect has been to discourage people from building to the IOR, and has led to the development of One-designs for offshore racing.

The earliest One-designs were the classes of dinghies that sprang up in the latter part of the nineteenth century. Larger wooden classes had followed, such as the *South Coast One-designs (SCODs)* and *Virtues* in Britain, and the *Folkboat* in Germany. The arrival of glass reinforced plastics boosted the development of One-designs. Since all the boats are identical and have the same equipment and sails, the only factor that can affect a race is the ability of the crew, unlike the ton-raters, where there are differences in design. Initially the small numbers of One-designs meant that the boats frequently sailed in the IOR races, but as they increased, class associations were formed, usually with the active encouragement of the manufacturers, and they ran their own events.

Above: An aerial view of an ocean-going yacht reaching under spinnaker. The crewman handling the sheet can be seen by the mast.

Right: An ocean-going trimaran reaching in very light weather. The crew of five would be the maximum a yacht of this size would want to carry.

Another move to avoid the inconvenience of handicapping has been to establish classes for boats of a particular length. This was started by the short-handers, who measured their classes in overall lengths, such as a class for boats between 45 and 50 feet (13.73 to 15.25 m). However, a group of owners sailing yachts rating roughly 40 feet under the IOR, found that all their boats were almost exactly 50 feet (15.25 m) in length and decided to race on an equal basis. The result was far more exciting sailing, and this 50-footer class is very popular. The major benefit is that a designer can produce a boat that does not have to be squeezed into a handicap rule, but which can be built for out and out speed. Perhaps the best example of this effect was when Philippe Jeantot, alone in his 60-footer (18.3 m) *Credit Agricole*, sailed past a fully crewed Maxi yacht of more than 75 feet (22.88 m) in length, as he approached Sydney at the end of the second leg of the 1986 BOC Challenge. *Credit Agricole* was designed for speed within 60 feet (18.3 m), while the Maxi had been built to succeed on handicap under the IOR.

Whilst many offshore sailors could feel the attraction of short-handed racing, there were limited numbers who actually wished to single-hand. In 1966 a new type of short-handed race was instituted by the Royal Western Yacht Club, and it appealed to everyone who liked a hard strenuous sail. This was the Two-Handed Round Britain and Ireland Race, from Plymouth, calling at: Cork in Eire; Barra in the outer Hebrides off the west coast of Scotland; Lerwick in the Shetland Islands; then sailing down the North Sea to Lowestoft and finally back to Plymouth. The rules were simple: two-handed; outside every island in the British Isles except the Channel Islands and Rockall; and each crew must take at least forty-eight hours break in each of the stop-over ports. The race, which draws up to a hundred international entrants, has been run every four years since (except for a three-year gap between 1982 and 1985 to adjust to the international schedule). It is significant that, apart from the second race in 1970 won by the 71-foot (21.66 m)

Crossbow, MacAlpine-Downie's successful design to break the world sailing speed record at Weymouth in 1980. She achieved a speed of over 36 knots.

The modern multihull such as *Spirit of Apricot* can achieve speeds three times as fast as a conventional yacht.

monohull *Ocean Spirit*, sailed by the author and Leslie Williams, the race has always gone to a multihull, despite the very mixed weather conditions that prevail around the British Isles. The author won again in 1974 in the 70-foot (21.34 m) catamaran *British Oxygen*, then the largest racing multihull ever built, and from that time onwards no one involved has seriously doubted the speed superiority of multihulls over monohulls.

The quest for even more challenging ocean races led to the creation of a fully crewed around-the-world race in 1973 for yachts built to the IOR rule. Co-ordinated by the Royal Naval Sailing Association of Britain and sponsored by the brewers Whitbread, it departed from Portsmouth, England, in August 1973, with stops at Cape Town, Sydney and Rio de Janeiro. The logistical problems of sailing a large yacht with full crew on a race in which each leg was nearly ten times a Fastnet Race were considerable. Ocean racing took on a new meaning as the crews battled with the Roaring Forties and learned that, in this event at least, the winner had to be a survivor as well as a good sailor. As with long-distance single-handed racing, the important factor was to achieve a good average speed and not break anything vital on the boat. The race was won by the Mexican entry *Sayula*, which although not crossing the line first, won on handicap. A comparable race was organized for 1975, but with only one stop in Sydney. This was called the *Financial Times* Clipper Race, since the objective was to prove that a modern yacht could circumnavigate the world faster than the old clipper ships. Only four boats entered and it was won by *Great Britain II*.

A pattern has emerged in the long-distance events, with the races being run in four-year cycles, and although the *Financial Times* Race was not repeated, the Whitbread Round the World Race was held again in 1977, 1981, 1985 and 1989. Each time the competition became more intense as people gained confidence from previous experience, and pushed their boats harder. Auckland replaced Sydney after the first race but otherwise only modest changes were made to the course until 1989, when Cape Town was deleted. At the same time the course was lengthened and now goes from Portsmouth to Punta del Este in Uruguay, then on to Fremantle, Auckland, eastwards to Punta del Este, Fort Lauderdale and finally back to Portsmouth.

Another short-handed race was introduced in 1975 by the Royal Cornwall Yacht Club, called the AZAB (the Azores and back), in which the boat may be sailed single- or two-handed. Like other events, it takes place every four years and has up to eighty entrants.

The contemporary practice of sponsors paying to have their advertising or name on a boat commenced rather half-heartedly in the 1960s, but by the early 1980s a new breed of professional sailor arrived on the scene who made his living by finding sponsors to fund a boat and crew. Because the International Yacht Racing Union, the world authority, continued until very recently to veto sponsors' logos on boats, these sailors entered events where this restriction did not apply, mainly the long-distance short-handed races such as the OSTAR, the French transatlantic single-handed race La Route de Rhum, and the Round Britain Race. In France, television was quick to appreciate the public's interest in seeing colourful, closely fought racing, and this exposure fuelled the sponsorship. Sponsors such as British Airways, Olympus Cameras and Gauloise were keen to fund fast boats that were newsworthy and had a chance of winning. By the mid-1980s, in response to demand, a whole series of new races had been added to the 'open' calendar. Because it was the source of greatest media attention, the races were mostly based in France, such as the La Baule to Dakar in French West Africa, Quebec to St. Malo, La Rochelle to New Orleans and the Round Europe Race. The initial Round Europe Race started in Kiel in 1985 and finished in Sardinia, having called at eight European countries. Unlike all other yachting events, these races have introduced prize money for the winners.

Cote d'Or of Belgium, skippered by Eric Tabarly, leaving the Solent at the start of the 1985 Whitbread Round the World Race.

Opposite: *Italia*, the Italian 12-metre entry for the America's Cup in 1986, splitting her spinnaker during the elimination series at Fremantle.

Inevitably, as the competition increased in this professional theatre, more and more of the skippers turned to multihulls because of their extra speed. The principle of the multihull is that it compensates for not having a heavy keel to keep itself upright by having a wide platform. It thus has enormous initial stability, but, without a keel, can be built much lighter than a similar sized monohull and will therefore normally be faster because it has less weight to push through the water.

The old sailing principle that a good big one will always beat a good little one still holds good, and the multihulls became longer. The first of the modern ocean-going multihulls was *Pen Duick IV*, built for Eric Tabarly, which subsequently sailed around the world; and by 1974 the catamaran *British Oxygen*, designed by Rod Macalpine-Downie, had demonstrated that the engineering was now almost complete for really large vessels of this type.

Today's ocean-racing multihull is a very speedy machine, having as good a windward performance as a monohull of equal size, but being considerably faster off the wind. The largest boats reached 85 feet (25.9 m) in length by the mid-1980s and cost close to a million pounds. They are capable of reaching 30 knots in bursts, and can average nearly 20 knots across an ocean. Sailing records that had stood since the time of the clipper ships began to tumble. The transatlantic record under sail, measured from the Ambrose Light Tower off New York to the Lizard Lighthouse in Cornwall, England, had remained at just over twelve days since the schooner *Atlantic* had bettered all previous times in 1905. In the 1970s this record was beaten by a trimaran, and by 1987 it had been reduced to seven days, six hours and thirty minutes by Frenchman Serge Medoc.

The search for ever increasing speeds, and the employment of materials such as carbon fibre in hull construction, and wing masts which resemble a vertical aircraft wing, unavoidably pushed prices to a point where even large company sponsors began to balk, and limits had to be put on overall length. 75 feet (22.88 m) is now the top length for racing, but the trend is towards 60 feet (18.3 m) as the maximum. Another money-saving device was the introduction of a Formula Forty, in which the boats are limited to 40 feet (12.2 m). This sponsored class sails in competitions around Europe and in the United States, providing exciting sailing close inshore where the races can be viewed by the public. Most races heretofore may have started and finished close to the shore, but the main portion of the race was out at sea where spectators could not see how the race was developing.

As the cost of building racing monohulls has also risen, owner pressure has ultimately forced the International Yacht Racing Union to agree to remove the restrictions on sponsorship of yachts for major international events such as the Admiral's Cup. Sponsors are paying for publicity, and since this can only be obtained by good results, there is now a market in this field for skilled professional crews who can produce a winning performance. The wheel has turned full circle, the professional of the nineteenth century slowly faded out as the wealthy owners found they could no longer afford huge yachts, but now with the arrival of sponsors and hence larger yachts, a professional yachtsman has re-emerged. The difference between the two eras is that in the meantime yachting has spread to encompass a vast new range of amateur owners, who, unaffected by commercial pressures, now provide the backbone of racing and cruising.

The America's Cup

The America's Cup in some ways dominates the sport of yachting. It has been in existence since 1851, and no other international sporting trophy has remained in the same hands for so long. The boats used for the races show the development of the yacht since the beginning of serious racing. From the outset it was seen very differently on each side of the Atlantic. The British tended to see it as an individual's attempt to wrest the Cup from the Americans, whereas the Americans have always viewed the competition as a national challenge.

Over the years, the conditions of the series have evolved. After the first race around the Isle of Wight in 1851, the Cup was taken to America and held by the New York Yacht Club. As the holders, the club could set the course of any subsequent challenge over ground of their choosing, and the New York Yacht Club considered it quite natural to take any advantage, such as refusing to have a deep water course because their own boat had a centreboard, and could sail across shallow waters inaccessible to the challenger with her fixed keel.

In the first two series in 1870 and 1871, the British challenger found herself facing a large number of defenders, but by 1876 it had been agreed a proper match race between one challenger and one defender would decide the issue in future, on a best of three race series. By 1895 this had been extended to the best of five, and in 1930 to the current best of seven. Courses were originally laid off New York, but in 1930 moved to Newport, Rhode Island, partly to avoid the commercial traffic, but also because Newport had become the summer vacationland for New York society.

The popular appeal of the America's Cup lies in the simplicity of the racing. The public does not have to understand a complicated handicap formula, because the boat in front is winning, and the races take place over a short course and are usually over within a few hours. Unlike many modern sporting competitions, the trophy for the winner is only an eighteenth-century silver cup, and there is no prize money.

In 1962 the challenge came in from Australia, led by Sir Frank Packer under the auspices of the Royal Sydney Yacht Squadron. The Australian team chartered *Vim* to

12-metres off Fremantle. The weather was much more robust than in Newport, and most teams moved there early to get used to the conditions.

Soudade, a member of the German Admiral's Cup team, running under a lightweight spinnaker during this closely fought series in 1987.

Opposite: *Yeoman XXII*, one of a long line of similarly named yachts, owned by the Aisher family, racing during Cowes Week.

gain experience whilst they built their own boat *Gretel*, and then started an exhaustive work-up under skipper Jock Sturrock. Only one new boat was produced in the United States, *Nefertiti*. She was lighter than any previous 12-metre (weighing only 57,500 lbs – 26,050 kgs, as against *Columbia's* 59,200 lbs – 26,820 kgs), with a beam of 13 feet (3.97 m). She started out well, winning ten of her first twelve races, but a greatly improved *Weatherly*, skippered by Bus Mosbacher, emerged as the best boat at the end of extensive trials.

This was the most exciting series since 1934. Although the Americans won, *Gretel* had the satisfaction of taking the second race, and might well have been more fortunate had there been stronger winds, as she seemed the better boat under these conditions. Certainly she could foot faster than *Weatherly*, although she was unable to point as close to the wind. Part of the problem may have lain in the constant changing of the crew by Packer, who – like many before, and after – found the temptation to meddle in the running of the boat irresistible.

The British had been just too late with their challenge for 1962, but were first in for 1964 with a new boat for Tony Boyden named *Sovereign*, from *Sceptre's* designer, David Boyd. There was not sufficient time to develop a second newly-designed British boat, so a near sister, *Kurrewa V*, was built by the Livingston brothers to act as another contender. The trials were close, but were won by *Sovereign*, skippered by Sir Peter Scott.

Two new boats were produced in America, *Constellation*, designed by the very experienced Olin Stephens for the Gubelmann syndicate, and *American Eagle*, by Luders for the Du Pont syndicate. Thus Tony Boyden found himself individually taking on a challenge that was to be defended by syndicates which included some of the wealthiest men in America. *Constellation*, skippered by Bob Bavier, showed herself to be the faster boat and was selected to defend.

Stars and Stripes and *Kiwi Magic* in 1987.

The first race took place in medium winds, and *Constellation* proved to be a much superior boat close to the wind, winning by five minutes. The British were left to pin their hopes on their boat having a good heavy-weather performance. They did not have to wait long; the second race was cancelled because the wind was below the limit of four knots, but it was blowing at twenty knots when the race was eventually sailed. The outcome was disastrous for the challengers. The Americans won by over twenty minutes, the largest margin since *Mayflower* beat *Galatea* in 1886. Although in the next two races the gap was never as wide, six and a half and fifteen minutes, the results for the British were depressing. It appeared that in nearly all sections of the contest the Americans were paramount, but nowhere more so than in the power for any yacht – her sails.

Two Australian syndicates challenged for 1967. Packer had *Gretel* completely rebuilt below the waterline, but the revamped boat was no match for the newcomer, *Dame Pattie*, which was steered by Jock Sturrock and owned by a Melbourne syndicate. The Americans built one boat, *Intrepid*, again designed by Stephens for a syndicate led by Bill Strawbridge. The syndicate had started work on the project soon after the previous series, endorsing Olin Stephens's comment that the essence of advance in the design of 12-metres lay in the imperceptible improvements in design and the work of a lot of people; and, in particular, the time to develop the boat's performance on the water. *Intrepid*, skippered by Bus Mosbacher, beat an improved *Constellation* to become the defender, and then won the series against the Australians by winning the first four races. The Americans had won again, and the Cup remained in the New York Yacht Club, bolted to its special table.

Australia had now succumbed totally to the America's Cup bug, and challenged again for 1970. So, too, did Britain, France and Greece. In order to stimulate competition, the New York Yacht Club suggested that the challengers hold a series of elimination trials in Newport, the winner to take on the chosen defender. This novel but sensible idea was agreed to, but the British and Greek challengers withdrew through lack of funds. The trials were close, and, had Baron Bich, the sporting head of the French challenge, not constantly changed his helmsman, his yacht *France* might well have won, but the Australian *Gretel II*, helmed by Jim Hardy, came through. Bill Ficker won the American trials with *Intrepid*.

The initial race was a disaster for the Australians; they broke a spinnaker pole and then lost more time recovering a crewman who had fallen overboard. The American yacht won, but both boats crossed the line flying protest flags, something not seen since 1934, although both protests were later dismissed. The second race caused more friction, as the boats collided shortly after the start, and although *Gretel II* won, the subsequent enquiry awarded the race to *Intrepid*. All hell broke loose when the results were made known. The New York Yacht Club was accused of being partial, and Packer threatened to go to the Supreme Court. The committee's decision was, in fact, quite right, however the uproar did lead to one reform to the race conditions. It was agreed that in future an international jury should hear protests, rather than the New York Yacht Club, who, whatever the truth, could hardly defend themselves against a claim of partisanship! The Americans took the third race, and were set to win the fourth when the wind shifted ninety degrees to favour the Australians, who won by just over a minute. What turned out to be the last race was sailed in light airs, and provided the spectators with a delightful and intensely fought contest, but the Americans' knowledge of the local wind conditions, and, in fairness, the cunning of their skipper, gave them a narrow victory.

The America's Cup had never been so popular, and no less than five countries now challenged, Australia, France, Britain, Canada and Italy, but when the series took place in 1974 only France and Australia actually appeared. Baron Bich's *France* lost the

Dennis Conner, the most successful America's Cup skipper in recent years, beaming as he regains the cup in Fremantle in January 1987.

Yachts in the 1989 America's Cup, with *New Zealand* in the foreground.

Opposite: Marc Pajot's *French Kiss*, the French challenger in Fremantle in the 1987 series, leading.

elimination series four-nil to the Australian challenge, which had come from the Royal Perth Yacht Club, backed by a property developer, Alan Bond. His new 12-metre, *Southern Cross*, designed by Bob Miller, was aluminium, which saved approximately fifteen per cent in hull weight, thus making it possible to add the remaining weight as ballast to make the boat stiffer. She was worked up strenuously against the two *Gretels*, which he had purchased, and she provided one of the best prepared challenges to date. Bond showed early signs that he was not the least impressed with the dignity and reputation of the New York Yacht Club. He enlivened proceedings considerably by announcing that he intended to run a video-tape recorder aboard *Southern Cross* to register any rule infringements, and he added that he was taking a lawyer with him to Newport!

The New York Yacht Club had its problems acquiring a defender but eventually two new boats were built, and after extensive trials one of them, *Courageous*, beat the well-tried *Intrepid*. Such were the complexities of crewing at the time that no less than three helmsmen were appointed, sailmaker Ted Hood for the windward legs, previous defender Bob Bavier for the downwind ones, and Dennis Conner to make the starts. The combination proved unbeatable, and they won in four straight races.

A number of small changes were made to the construction rules between the 1974 and 1977 series, with the objective of making the 12-metres more seaworthy, and, it was hoped, to give them an alternative life as ocean racers. In 1977 two challenges came from Australia, and one each from France, Sweden and Britain. The British one again did not materialize through lack of funds. The elimination series between the challenging nations was won by *Australia*. The outcome of the American trials was unexpected. Ted Turner was offered *Courageous* to provide competition for Ted Hood's *Independence*. Turner said that he would sail the boat and pay all the costs, provided the boat was his to race if he won the trials. Turner has a brash personality, and perhaps it was hoped that Hood in the newer boat would win. Turner won the elimination series, and, in the event, these were more exciting than the real thing, which *Courageous* won in four straight races. However, the divide between the challengers and defenders was narrowing, as the greatest margin was only two and a half minutes.

No place for weak muscles! The cockpit of *Kiwi Magic* in the 1987 series.

A moment of Cup history. John Bertrand, skipper of *Australia II*, at the finish of the deciding seventh race in the 1983 America's Cup.

The British experimental 12-metre, being prepared for shipment to Australia in 1986. Although she showed potential, she arrived too late to be worked up properly.

Alan Bond challenged again for 1980 with a new boat called *Australia I*, designed by Ben Lexcen (who had been the Bob Miller of Miller and Whitworth). An elimination series disposed of the other challengers: the British *Lionheart* organization led by Tony Boyden, and the Italian *Azzurra* syndicate. The American selection was *Freedom* sailed by Dennis Conner. This time the races were even closer. *Freedom* won the first race by two minutes, and then *Australia I* took the second by half a minute. The next race went to the Americans by a minute, and then the others by four and three minutes. Much of the success of the defence must be attributed to Conner's more professional approach, and in his team, at least, the America's Cup races finally lost any resemblance to the pretence of the gentlemanly sport from which they had evolved, and were now treated almost as a fight to the death. Despite this attitude the Australians had come very near indeed, and the final gap between the participants, which had always appeared unbridgeable, was now nearly closed.

Alan Bond and his team had learned much from 1980, and returned to Newport for the next confrontation in 1983, not only with a superbly trained team and a new boat from Lexcen, *Australia II*, but with a cupboard-full of psychological tricks to unnerve the opposition. But first they had to defeat the other challengers, six in all. Cup fever was everywhere. People perhaps sensed that the Americans could at last be beaten, and everyone wanted to be in for the kill. The largest contingent came from Australia. In addition to *Australia II* there were two other syndicated yachts, *Advance* and *Challenge 12*. The French brought over *France 3*, the Canadians *Canada I*, the Italians *Azzurra*, from a syndicate that included the Aga Khan, and from Britain came *Victory 83*, backed by Peter De Savary. The seriousness of these challenges may be indicated by the example of the British team, which trained in Newport during the summer before the series, and then went south to the Bahamas to continue practising throughout the winter.

Such a host of challengers led to a long and tough elimination series, which did much to raise the crewing of the boats involved to the high standards that the American trials had always given the defenders. The initial trials eliminated *Advance*, *Challenge 12* and *France 3*, and the semi-finals *Azzurra* and *Canada I*. *Victory 83* and *Australia II* now had a mini Cup series, which the Australians won 4-1. Bond's careful planning had paid off, and his team had a momentum that would be hard to stop. The Americans

realized the danger, and a crop of successful sailors vied to defend, each ready even to have his head replace the Cup in the event of losing the series, as one member of the New York Yacht Club had threatened! Dennis Conner's syndicate had three new boats, *Liberty*, *Magic* and *Spirit of America*. *Defender* and *Courageous* were entered by another syndicate, but *Liberty* proved to be the ablest of the five.

Whilst these trials were under way, the usual America's Cup wrangles focused on the peculiar winged keel fitted to *Australia II*. The keel was worrying the Americans, not least because *Australia II* had shown herself to be very fast and well sailed. As if to create a mystery, the Australians frustrated every effort to inspect the keel by keeping it shrouded. The Americans claimed that the keel was unfair and furthermore it had been designed in Holland, and not by Lexcen, as required by the rules. The Australian challengers seemed to have been waiting for this response, and not only established that the Dutch patent was held by Lexcen, but that the American defenders themselves had only that summer tried to persuade the Dutch research centre to work on a winged keel – so they had no grounds for complaint. The Americans were forced to accept the situation regarding the keel, which not only made *Australia II* the most manoeuvrable 12-metre to date, it also gave the Australians a considerable psychological advantage.

To the strains of 'The Empire Strikes Back', Conner's *Liberty* was towed out from her dock in Newport on 14 September 1983 for her confrontation with *Australia II*, skippered by John Bertrand, whose loudspeakers blared 'I come from a land down-under/ where women glow and men plunder'. At noon, the ten-minute preparation gun fired, and precisely ten minutes and three seconds later *Australia II* crossed the line, three seconds ahead of *Liberty*. The Americans commenced a tacking duel on the first leg to test the Australian boat's much vaunted manoeuvrability, but finding it to be a fact, soon gave up. The next two sections of the triangular Olympic-style course were reaching legs, and *Liberty* demonstrated that at least in reaching she was the speedier boat, and she took the lead. The Australians came back on the run, being faster than imagined, but just towards the end of the leg had a steering failure which allowed the Americans through – and to win by seventy seconds.

The second race went to the Americans by one minute and thirty-three seconds, owing to a problem with the Australians' mainsail. The third race ran out of time with the Australians well in the lead, a fact that seemed to rebuild any loss in confidence they might have been feeling, and they won the fourth by two minutes and forty-seven seconds. When Conners won the fifth by forty-three seconds to make the score 3-1, he needed only one more victory to retain the Cup. Despite having a faster boat, it looked as if *Australia II* was to be relegated to the history books as yet another challenger which nearly made it. However, although she had to win all the three races remaining, luck for once was on the challenger's side. Before the start of the sixth race the Americans had a rigging failure, and although they managed to make temporary repairs, their performance was affected and they trailed at the finish line by one minute and forty-seven seconds. In the seventh race the Australians won by three minutes and twenty-five seconds to square the series, with one race outstanding.

The final race was bound to be an epic. Both teams headed out brim-full of assurance, the Americans sure that they would win, and the Australians certain that they would be making history. *Liberty* led at the end of the first leg, and stretched this on the first reach, but the Australians came back on the second. On the fourth leg, a beat, *Liberty* again extended her advantage, but lost it all plus twenty-one seconds to *Australia II* on the run. Having taken the lead, the Australians hung onto it, and came in first by forty-one seconds. At last, the America's Cup was bound for a destination other than the New York Yacht Club, where it had been for the previous 132 years. Australia celebrated by declaring a national holiday.

The semi-finalists fight it out to challenge for the cup in Fremantle. *Stars and Stripes* and *Kiwi Magic*.

Previous page: Fremantle Harbour Western Australia, scene of the America's Cup in 1987.

The Royal Perth Yacht Club, now the proud owners of the Cup, were quick to make the most of their fame, and announced the next series would be early in 1987 off Fremantle, Australia, where the wind was stronger and the seas were greater than anything experienced in Newport. The Americans, determined to regain what they considered to be their property, entered no less than four syndicates, and there were challenges from Canada, Britain, France, Italy and New Zealand. All the teams went to Fremantle in plenty of time to become familiar with the conditions, and a complicated series of trials and eliminations were run to allow the best challenger to come forward. This was to be Dennis Conner in *Stars and Stripes*, under the auspices of the San Diego Yacht Club, after a final tussle with the first glass-fibre 12-metre, *Kiwi Magic*, from New Zealand. The Australian defenders also had four syndicates from which to select, including that of Alan Bond, but the right was won by Iain Murray's *Kookaburra*. The actual Cup races were an anticlimax after the strenuous series of the challengers and defenders, and Conner won four straight races to return the Cup to the United States – but to San Diego not New York.

The next contest should have followed in 1989 but a New Zealand banker, Michael Fay, decided to enter early a challenge based upon the original deeds, which restricted the competitor's boat to a waterline of 115 feet (35.08 m) if two-masted and 90 feet (27.45 m) if rigged with a single mast. His giant entry, *New Zealand*, had a waterline length of 90 feet (27.45 m) and was 133 feet (40.57 m) overall, with a beam of 26 feet (7.93 m) so that the forty-man crew could apply their weight as far outboard as possible to provide stability. The Americans consulted their lawyers, and responded with a 60-foot (18.3m) catamaran, which was challenged by the New Zealanders. Quite how anyone thought that a match between a monohull, even one as large as *New Zealand*, and a modern multihull, could be fair is beyond reason, but Conner managed to convince the courts of his case, and the best of three series in 1988 in San Diego was a boring procession. Subsequently the New York Supreme Court ruled that the multihull was illegal, and awarded the Cup to New Zealand, but this is being appealed.

If this challenge did nothing else, it maintained the reputation of the America's Cup for incurring acrimonious charges of cheating between the opponents, and it certainly added no lustre to the great event. After the San Diego fiasco there was a meeting of interested parties to agree the type of boat for future Cup competitions. The 12-metre class is to be dropped, and in future the America's Cup will be sailed in a new 75-foot (22.88 m) boat, the series to be held in either March 1991 in New Zealand or September 1991 in San Diego, depending upon the outcome of the latest court battles.

The Olympics

The Olympics are now sailed in dinghies and small keelboats, with the largest boat being the *Soling*. From time to time there have been suggestions that larger boats, such as are used for ocean racing, might be included, but the general view is that these would cost too much to build and campaign for the less wealthy nations, and the Olympic objective is, after all, to allow the best from each country to participate.

The 1960 Olympics were held in Italy, and the yachting was in the Bay of Naples. Five classes were involved, the *Star*, *Dragon*, *Finn*, *5.5 metre*, and a new boat designed by Van Essen of Holland called the *Flying Dutchman*. This centreboard two-man dinghy, measuring 19 feet 10 inches (6.05 m) in length, proved a very lively and exciting boat to race, and with the crewman out on the trapeze they have been clocked at 11 knots. Norway took the gold for the class in Naples, with the other classes going respectively

Kiwi Magic at Fremantle which was beaten by *Stars and Stripes* for the position of challenger in the 1987 America's Cup.

Flying Dutchman dinghies at the 1984
Los Angeles Olympic Games.

to the Soviet Union, Greece, Denmark and the United States, from a total of forty-six competing nations. In these games the Dane Paul Elvström clocked up his third successive Olympic win in the *Finn* class, a record which still stands.

The identical classes were used four years later in Tokyo, where forty nations took part, the gold medals going to the Bahamas for the *Star*, to Denmark for the *Dragon*, West Germany for the *Finn*, Australia for the *5.5 metre*, and New Zealand for the *Flying Dutchman*. At Acapulco in 1968, the United States won the *Star* and the *Dragon*, the Soviet Union the *Finn*, Sweden the *5.5 metre* and Great Britain the *Flying Dutchman*, skippered by Rodney Pattisson and crewed by Iain MacDonald-Smith.

The 1972 Olympics at Kiel in West Germany brought forty-eight competing countries to the games, the greatest number so far, and saw three changes to the line-up of yachts. The *5.5 metre* was retired and in its place came the three-man *Soling* designed by the Norwegian Jan Herman Linge. It has a fixed keel and measures 26 feet 9 inches (8.5 m) overall. An extra class was added, the *Tempest*, a two-man keelboat 21 feet $11\frac{1}{2}$ inches (6.7 m) long, designed by Ian Proctor in Britain. The *Tempest* was designated as the successor to the *Star*, but both classes competed at Kiel. The Australians won the *Star* and *Dragon* gold medals, France the *Finn*, Rodney Pattisson of Britain the *Flying Dutchman* again, the United States the *Soling*, and the Soviet Union the *Tempest* class.

There were three more alterations for the 1976 Olympics at Kingston in Canada, the *Star* and the *Dragon* were dropped, and a two-man centreboard dinghy, the *470* introduced. For the first time a lightweight multihull, the *Tornado*, made an appearance. Twenty-eight nations competed, the West Germans being the most successful, with gold medals in the *Flying Dutchman* and *470*. Rodney Pattisson had to console himself with a silver in the *Flying Dutchman*, thereby just missing out on equalling Paul Elvström's

Randy Smyth and Jay Glaser of America, who were first in the *Tornado* class in the Los Angeles Olympic Games, 1984.

Below, left: The *Soling* class *Searcher One*, an Olympic three-man keelboat class.

Flying Dutchman class dinghy.

Rodney Pattisson of England, who won two golds and a silver in three successive Olympics in the *Flying Dutchman* class.

Above, right: Luis Doreste and Roberto Molina of Spain who won the *470* class in Los Angeles.

Below: Paul Elvström in Fremantle, Western Australia.

record in one class. East Germany won the *Finn*, Denmark the *Soling*, Sweden the *Tempest* and Great Britain the *Tornado*. Unfortunately, only twenty-eight nations attended, the smallest turn-out for twenty years. Part of the problem was that although efforts were being made to keep down the costs of Olympic classes by choosing smaller boats to ensure the widest possible participation, the boats themselves were becoming very technical and therefore more expensive.

In 1980 the Olympics took place in the Soviet Union, but in response to the invasion of Afghanistan many nations boycotted the games, and the sailing at Tallinn in Estonia was particularly affected, with only twenty-one nations present. The only change in the boat line-up was the reintroduction of the *Star* class at the expense of the *Tempest*. The *Soling* was won by Denmark, the *Star* by the Soviet Union, giving Valentin Mankin his second gold medal, as he had previously won the *Flying Dutchman* in Kingston. The *470* and *Tornado* gold medals went to Brazil, and the *Finn* appropriately enough to Finland.

A new class was inaugurated four years later in 1984 at Los Angeles. This was the *Windglider*, a form of surfboard with a mast and sail, which reflected the increasing enthusiasm for this type of inexpensive sailing. Although there was a reciprocal boycott of these games by many Communist countries, the *Windglider* class attracted thirty-eight entrants and was won by Holland. The United States won the *Soling*, *Star* and *Flying Dutchman* classes, New Zealand the *Tornado* and *Finn*, Spain the *470*.

The sailing events in the Olympic Games in 1988 at Pusan in South Korea were the most popular ever, with no less than forty-five nations taking part. For the first time a separate class for women was arranged, and they sailed against each other in *470* dinghies. The medals were well spread, New Zealand winning the *Windglider*, France the men's *470* and *Tornado*, East Germany the *Soling*, the United States the women's *470*, Jose Doreste of Spain the *Finn* to give him his second gold in two games, Denmark the *Flying Dutchman*, and Britain the *Star*. An additional boat is being added for the 1992 Barcelona games in Spain, the *Europe* single-handed dinghy for women, plus a women's sailboard class, which brings the total number of classes to nine.

The first single-handed circumnavigator, Joshua Slocum, aboard *Spray* in 1907.

Previous page: Brighton Marina, England.

Single-Handing

Single-handing has always had its adherents. For some it is the opportunity to get away from people for a while, for others a chance to test themselves in all the disciplines that are required to make a voyage, whether cruising or racing. In crewed racing in recent years there has been a tendency for specialized roles, so that a boat carries a navigator, a helmsman, sailtrimmer, tactician, and so on, all experts in their particular field. A single-hander needs all these qualifications, but additionally has to be a consummate master of the most important quality of all – seamanship.

The second single-handed transatlantic race (OSTAR) took place in 1964 with only one change, the finishing line was moved from New York to Newport, Rhode Island. All the five entrants from the 1960 race re-entered, together with ten other contestants. The main interest in the race focused on the three multihulls, *Rehu Moana*, owned by David Lewis, Mike Butterfield's *Misty Miller*, and *Folâtre*, sailed by Derek Kelsall. Few people considered these boats to be safe for an ocean crossing. The same view was taken about a lightweight monohull *Pen Duick II* entered by a French naval officer, Eric Tabarly, which, at 44 feet (13.42 m) overall, was judged too large to be managed by one man alone. In the event, Tabarly won in twenty-seven days, three hours and fifty-six minutes, beating Francis Chichester by two days and twenty hours. Only one of the fifteen starters failed to finish. The last boat to arrive, *Marco Polo* sailed by Axel Pederson, was at sea for sixty-three days.

This race had two effects. Primarily, the safe outcome again confirmed single-handing as an acceptable adventure sport and one which captured the popular imagination – the public liked the idea of lone sailors racing across a dangerous ocean. Secondly, Tabarly's victory, much respected by the British, gave sailing, and single-handing in particular, a tremendous boost in his native France and was to inspire many excellent young French sailors to take to the sea.

Before the next planned OSTAR, a voyage of great significance, the penultimate single-handed undertaking, was made by Francis Chichester. Convinced from his crossings of the Atlantic that safe, long-distance, single-handed passages were feasible, Chichester, at the age of sixty-five, decided to discover if he could sail around the world and beat the times set by the clipper ships. For the venture he commissioned a new boat, the 54-footer (16.47 m) *Gypsy Moth IV*. He sailed from Plymouth in England on

Four of the five competitors in the first *Observer* Single-Handed Transatlantic Race (OSTAR), from left: Francis Chichester, Blondie Hasler, David Lewis and Val Howells. The fifth competitor was Jean Lacombe.

Eric Tabarly, one of the most successful single-handers, who was responsible for the modern popularity of the sport in France.

Francis Chichester, the first of the modern single-handed circumnavigators.

Below, right: Alec Rose waving a tankard as he returns to Portsmouth at the end of his circumnavigation on 4 July 1968.

27 August 1966, and followed the traditional clipper track down the Atlantic and into the awesome Roaring Forties of the Southern Ocean. (The name refers to the southern latitude of forty degrees, where the wind and seas roll uninterrupted around the globe, save for a small tip of land at Cape Horn.) He sailed eastwards to Australia where he stopped for repairs and a rest, but he had already completed the longest solo passage in history. When he recovered, he departed for England, taking the arduous route around Cape Horn, and arriving back in Plymouth on 28 May 1967. It was an outstanding feat, and one for which the sailor was justifiably knighted upon his return.

Another Englishman and veteran of the 1964 transatlantic race, Alec Rose, intended to leave in his 36-foot (10.98 m) yacht, *Lively Lady*, at the same time as Chichester, but an accident to his boat necessitated a year's delay. In 1967 he sailed non-stop to Australia, but on the homeward passage was forced into Bluff in New Zealand for repairs. With these effected, he set out again and finished his voyage on 4 July 1968.

Single-handing was news, and two events in 1968 ensured its continued prominence. On 1 June the next *Observer* transatlantic race began, this time with thirty-five starters, including Eric Tabarly. Compared with previous races, this one was a disaster, as only nineteen finished, although fortunately no lives were lost. Just five of the thirteen multihulls finished, but from the outset some of the boats looked decidedly experimental. The winner was Geoffrey Williams of Britain in a new 56-foot (17.1 m) ketch *Sir Thomas Lipton*, in a time of twenty-five days, twenty hours and thirty-three minutes. Bruce Dalling of South Africa came in second in *Voortrekker*, and for a while it looked as if he might be persuaded to file a protest against Williams, who had not rounded the Nantucket Lightship, a mark of the course, but he declined to do so.

Even as the OSTAR commenced, a much greater epic was getting under way — no less than a race around the world single-handed and non-stop. Chichester's and Rose's achievements had left only this feat to be accomplished, and it was inevitable that someone would attempt this within a year or two of their homecoming. In fact by the end of 1967 there were at least four people making plans, and early the next year the *Sunday Times* in London offered a trophy called the Golden Globe for the first person to make such a voyage, which was to start and finish at the same port in the British Isles. The increasing number of contestants made it impractical for them all to be herded together on a single day for a mass start, and the newspaper subsequently added another prize of £5,000, which would be awarded to the person who, starting at any time between June and October 1968, made the *fastest* non-stop circumnavigation.

Robin Knox-Johnston departing from Plymouth in *Suhaili*, the first boat to circumnavigate the world non-stop, at the start of the 1988 Single-Handed Transatlantic Race.

Opposite: Yachts of all types and sizes gather in Plymouth for the 1988 Carlsberg Single-Handed Transatlantic Race.

Eventually there were nine starters, six from Britain, two from France and one from Italy. The rules were simple. The boat, with only one person on board, should sail from a port in the British Isles around the world without receiving any assistance or calling into a port. Although no rule stated that it was necessary, all intended to take the traditional eastward route through the Roaring Forties, since the winds in the Southern Ocean blow from west to east. John Ridgway sailed on 1 June in his 30-foot (9.15 m) *English Rose IV*, Chay Blyth on 8 June in his 30-foot (9.15 m) bilge keeler *Dytiscus III*, and the author on 14 June in his 32-foot (9.76 m) ketch *Suhaili*, which he had built in India three years previously. All three set off early because they had small boats and therefore a comparatively slow speed, and they wanted to ensure they rounded Cape Horn in January, which is midsummer in the southern hemisphere. John Ridgway withdrew at Recife in Brazil after fifty-one days at sea, when his boat began to split at the deck; and Chay Blyth went to South Africa after ninety-eight days because he found his boat was unsafe in the Southern Ocean. On 21 August the next competitors set sail – a very experienced Frenchman, Bernard Moitessier, in a 39-foot (11.9 m) ketch *Joshua*, and a compatriot, Loick Fougeron, in a 30-foot (9.15 m) cutter *Captain Browne*. Fougeron retired off the Cape of Good Hope after storm damage, having been at sea for ninety-eight days. Bill King, a retired submarine commander, left Britain on 24 August in his specially built 42-foot (12.81 m) schooner *Galway Blazer*. He too suffered damage near the Cape of Good Hope, and pulled out after eighty-seven days. Nigel Tetley, another naval officer, sailed on 16 September in his 40-foot (12.2 m) trimaran *Victress*; Donald Crowhurst on 31 October in a similar trimaran *Teignmouth Electron*; and Alec Carozzo in a 68-foot (20.74 m) ketch *Gancia Americano*, also on 31 October. Carozzo became ill, and withdrew after twenty-six days.

Crowhurst pottered around the southern Atlantic, calling in at Argentina, and transmitting false progress reports, but before his dishonesty could be exposed, his boat was found floating empty in the north Atlantic. Three of the competitors managed to enter the Southern Ocean and round Cape Horn – the author, Bernard Moitessier, and Nigel Tetley. By sailing early the author had a sufficient head start to lead through the Roaring Forties, although plagued by the thought that such a voyage might be beyond his boat's capabilities, and he was the first around the Horn on 17 January 1969. He was followed on 5 February by Bernard Moitessier, who subsequently retired from the race on 18 March when lying some 1,500 miles behind the leader. The author sailed back into Falmouth on 22 April 1969 after 312 days at sea, the only finisher of the nine starters. The last possible major single-handed voyage had been completed.

'Blondie' Hasler's junk-rigged *Folkboat*, *Jester*, being sailed by Mike Richey in 1965.

Too big to be safe! The 246-foot *Club Méditerrannée*, which came second in the 1976 OSTAR.

Chay Blyth arriving home on 4 August 1971 after performing the first single-handed circumnavigation east to west.

Robin Knox-Johnston ashore for the first time after 312 days alone at sea, during which he completed the first non-stop circumnavigation of the world.

Almost a month later Tetley sent out a distress call near the Azores, as his trimaran was disintegrating. He was rescued after 246 days at sea. The distance he covered non-stop and his length of time at sea are still world records for a multihull. In November 1970 Chay Blyth tried again in a specially built 56-foot (17.08 m) steel ketch *British Steel*. He decided to sail around the world from east to west, a voyage he achieved in 292 days. A decade before, an Atlantic crossing had seemed the ultimate single-handed voyage; now the world had been circumnavigated in both directions single-handed.

Single-handing, despite the catalogue of male achievement so far, has an equal appeal for women. On 12 June 1971, a diminutive English lady, Nicolette Milnes-Walker, sailed in the 30-foot (9.15 m) sloop *Aziz* from Dale in Wales and arrived safely in Newport, Rhode Island, on 26 July, the first non-stop crossing of the Atlantic by a woman. Quite a few women have since completed the OSTAR. By 1972 the OSTAR was the leading single-handed racing event, and fifty-two boats started. Amongst these was a relative giant sailed by Jean Yves Terlain, *Vendredi 13*, 128 feet (39.04 m) in length and fitted with four masts from which self-tacking mainsails were set. The objective was to obtain the maximum waterline length, and therefore the maximum possible hull speed — for a monohull. (The waterline formula does not apply to multihulls.) In fact it was Tabarly's *Pen Duick IV*, but sailed by Alain Colas, that was to win in twenty days, thirteen hours and fifteen minutes, finishing sixteen hours ahead of her large rival. Forty of the starters arrived in Newport. Within a year Alain Colas had taken *Pen Duick IV* around the world with one stop, not beating Tetley's distance record, but proving that a multihull could attain a single-handed circumnavigation.

The 1976 OSTAR brought more entries, including an even longer monohull, *Club Méditerranée*, sailed by Alain Colas, which was 236 feet (71.98 m) in length. The boat was so enormous that a crew had to set the sails before the race got under way and then jump off, leaving the sailor to cope as best he could. 124 boats set out from Plymouth, of which seventy-five finished. The race was won by Eric Tabarly in a large but conventional monohull, mainly due to force 10 winds in the Atlantic which delayed or damaged the multihulls. Alain Colas's monster came second, but the question of safety concerning such a huge boat with only a single-handed crew aboard meant this was the last time boats of these dimensions would be permitted.

Credit Agricole sailed by Philippe Jeantot, the winner of the 1982 BOC Challenge Single-Handed Around The World Race.

Opposite: The hand-painted motif on Florence Arthaud's *Groupe Pierre Ier*.

Biscuit's Lu, a typical modern 60-foot single-handed ocean racer.

The following year the first attempt was made by a woman at a single-handed circumnavigation, when New Zealander Naomi James departed from Dartmouth, England, in a 53-foot (16.17 m) cutter *Express Crusader* on 9 September 1977. On 7 June 1978 she finished the voyage, having made stops in Cape Town and the Falklands. She holds the record for being the first woman to sail alone around Cape Horn. Her record for circumnavigation was beaten on 5 June 1988 when a thirty-four-year-old Australian, Kay Cottee, sailed into Sydney in her 37-footer (11.29 m), *Blackmores First Lady*, having sailed non-stop from Sydney the previous year, around Cape Horn, past the St. Peter and St. Paul Rocks north of the Equator, round the Cape of Good Hope, and back to Sydney in 189 days. Although this is nearly sixty days outside the record for a solo circumnavigation, it is the first one to be accomplished non-stop by a woman.

In 1978 La Route de Rhum was established, a new French single-handed transatlantic race from St. Malo to Guadeloupe in the West Indies, and this and the OSTAR have continued at four-yearly intervals ever since. Meanwhile, some single-handed sailors were beginning to search for a greater challenge, and their thoughts consequently turned to an around-the-world race, but this time with stop-overs in three ports along the way. The idea was picked up by the BOC Group, who asked the author to be chairman of the race committee, and agreed to sponsor the event, which became known as the BOC Challenge. The race was to start and finish in Newport, Rhode Island, with breaks in Cape Town, Sydney and Rio de Janeiro. In all, seventeen boats from ten different countries entered the first challenge, and ten completed the gruelling course. The race began in August 1982 and the winner was a Frenchman, Philippe Jeantot, in his 56-footer (17.08 m), *Credit Agricole*. Class 2, for 40-footers to 50-footers (12.2 to 15.25 m), was won by the Japanese Yuko Tada in *Koden Okera*. The BOC Challenge was repeated in 1986, and has become recognized as a classic single-handed race, to continue at four-yearly intervals.

This race helped to focus attention on a growing problem with single-handers: the maximum size of the boats they should be allowed to sail, bearing in mind that they must sleep sometimes and then they cannot keep a look-out for other shippping. In the small number of collisions that have taken place, it has always been the single-hander's yacht that has come off worst. But the giant boats have the potential to damage or even sink a fishing trawler or small coaster, and whereas the single-handers accept the risks, none wishes to endanger other people's lives. So a measure of agreement was reached between the BOC organizers, the Royal Western Yacht Club in England (responsible for the OSTAR), and the Goat Island Yacht Club in Newport in the United States (responsible for the Bermuda One-Two Race – single-handed from Newport to Bermuda, two-handed back) that 60 feet (18.3 m) would be the maximum length allowed in their single-handed races. This rule was also applied for the 1989 Globe Challenge, a single-handed non-stop around-the-world race organized in France.

Single-handers may be open to criticism since they obviously cannot comply with Rule 5 of the *International Regulations for Preventing Collisions at Sea*, which requires that all vessels should keep a permanent look-out. (In reply to such criticism one might point out that a collision is theoretically impossible, if even only one ship is keeping its proper look-out, since Rule 17 demands that if a vessel thinks another boat is not going to give way, it must give way itself.) But the sport of single-handing will continue to thrive. The 1989 Globe Challenge was the first of its kind for twenty-one years, and may well be added to the four-yearly cycle of races. There are people who go single-handing because a particular race stipulates that there should be only one person on board, and there are those who do it simply because they enjoy the experience and occasional periods of solitude with the sea. The races achieve the headlines, but cruising single-handed is as old as racing, and continues to draw a worldwide following.

Nicolette Milnes-Walker, the first woman to cross the Atlantic non-stop single-handed, shown with her stores the day before her departure in June 1971.

Australian Kay Cottee, who became the first woman to sail alone around the world non-stop in 1988.

The America's Cup
Winners

Year	Defender	Challenger	Winner
1851	Royal Yacht Squadron (UK)	*America* (USA)	*America*
1870	New York Yacht Club (USA)	*Cambria* (UK)	NYYC
1871	*Columbia/Sappho* (USA)	*Livonia* (UK)	NYYC
1876	*Madelaine* (USA)	*Countess of Dufferin* (Can)	*Madelaine*
1881	*Mischief* (USA)	*Atlanta* (Can)	*Mischief*
1885	*Puritan* (USA)	*Genesta* (UK)	*Puritan*
1886	*Mayflower* (USA)	*Galatea* (UK)	*Mayflower*
1887	*Volunteer* (USA)	*Thistle* (UK)	*Volunteer*
1893	*Vigilant* (USA)	*Valkyrie II* (UK)	*Vigilant*
1895	*Defender* (USA)	*Valkyrie III* (UK)	*Defender*
1899	*Columbia* (USA)	*Shamrock I* (UK)	*Columbia*
1901	*Columbia* (USA)	*Shamrock II* (UK)	*Columbia*
1903	*Reliance* (USA)	*Shamrock III* (UK)	*Reliance*
1920	*Resolute* (USA)	*Shamrock IV* (UK)	*Resolute*
1930	*Enterprise* (USA)	*Shamrock V* (UK)	*Enterprise*
1934	*Rainbow* (USA)	*Endeavour I* (UK)	*Rainbow*
1937	*Ranger* (USA)	*Endeavour II* (UK)	*Ranger*
1958	*Columbia* (USA)	*Sceptre* (UK)	*Colombia*
1962	*Weatherly* (USA)	*Gretel* (Aus)	*Weatherly*
1964	*Constellation* (USA)	*Sovereign* (UK)	*Constellation*
1967	*Intrepid* (USA)	*Dame Pattie* (Aus)	*Intrepid*
1970	*Intrepid* (USA)	*Gretel II* (Aus)	*Intrepid*
1974	*Courageous* (USA)	*Southern Cross* (Aus)	*Courageous*
1977	*Courageous* (USA)	*Australia* (Aus)	*Courageous*
1980	*Freedom* (USA)	*Australia I* (Aus)	*Freedom*
1983	*Liberty* (USA)	*Australia II* (Aus)	*Australia II*
1987	*Kookaburra* (Aus)	*Stars and Stripes* (USA)	*Stars and Stripes*
1989	*Stars and Stripes* (USA)	*New Zealand* (NZ)	Awaits decision

Rating

The objective of a rating system is to provide a means of allowing yachts of varying size and sail area to race against each other in such a way that their irregularities can be levelled by a handicap or time allowance calculated on the differences in their ratings. Over the years a number of different rating systems developed, with calculations based on the sail area and size and ratio of waterline length and beam of the yachts. These calculations became progressively more complicated in an attempt to achieve fair competition between different boats.

The rating system developed in the first half of the nineteenth century gave a time allowance based upon builders' measurements, which were the same measurements used for calculating the tonnage of merchant ships. Since it was calculated on a yacht's beam and keel length, it produced deep, long, narrow craft which could set as much sail as they dared. By 1854, it was realized that this was unsatisfactory, and a new rule was introduced by the Royal Thames and the Royal Mersey Yacht Clubs. However, it led to such an outcry from the owners of boats built to the earlier rule that it was modified to what is still applicable as the Thames Measurement of a yacht:

$$\frac{(\text{length} - \text{beam}) \times \text{beam} \times \frac{1}{2}\,\text{beam}}{94} = \text{tonnage}$$

This rule also penalized beam and did not take sail area into account, so yachts grew even slimmer, with longer bowsprits and counters. The ultimate rule cheater was the English yacht *Oona*, which had an overall length of 46 feet (14 m), a waterline length of 32 feet (9.7 m), a draft of 8 feet (2.44 m), and a beam of $5\frac{1}{2}$ feet (1.7 m).

A number of other rating systems were to be found elsewhere, and because this made racing between yachts built and measured to different rules complicated, a group of yachtsmen formed the Yacht Racing Association in 1875, with the objective of standardizing ratings and rules. Their rule, know as the YRA Tonnage Rule, was based on the formula:

$$\frac{(\text{length} + \text{beam})\,2 \times \text{beam}}{1,730} = \text{rating}$$

This rule had limited success, and led to the development of Raters, one of the best known being the Duke of York's one-rater *White Rose*. But in 1886 Dixon Kemp invented a new and improved rule which paid attention to two of the main factors that govern a yacht's speed:

$$\frac{\text{waterline length} \times \text{sail area}}{6,000} = \text{rating}$$

Some beautiful yachts were built to this rule, perhaps the most famous being the *Britannia*, but it was inadequate in some respects. A modification was introduced in 1896, known as the Linear Rating Rule, which lasted until 1905:

$$\frac{\text{length} + \text{beam} + \frac{3}{4}\,\text{girth} + \frac{1}{2}\,\text{sail area}}{2} = \text{rating in feet}$$

The advent of a new rule did not mean that all existing yachts were immediately disqualified: they were re-rated. But designers soon created boats that took advantage of the new rule and made it harder for the older boats to compete.

In 1904 America adopted the Universal Rule, conceived by Nathaniel Herreshoff, which labelled classes alphabetically. In 1906 thirteen European countries joined together to form the International Yacht Racing Union, which produced the International Rule. This was the first international standardized rating, and the different classes were defined in metres. There were ten classes in all, which lasted until World War II, but today only the 6, 8 and 12-metre classes exist. Unfortunately, America did not accept the metre classes until 1921, and in 1931 Europe adopted the Universal Rule for yachts measuring over 14.5 in the metre rule.

Between the two world wars, the Royal Ocean Racing Club Rule was commonly used for rating in Europe, and the Cruising Club of America's Rule was used in America. Both brought far more factors into the calculations in order to compare yachts in a more satisfactory manner, but they were not interchangeable. Finally, in 1970, a new system was introduced which provided one rule applicable worldwide, the International Offshore Rule, and this, plus its various modifications, governs offshore racing today. The IOR involves a large number of measurements of a yacht, but the basic formula is:

$$\frac{(0.13 \; L \times 2/S + 0.25L + 0.2 \; 2/S + DC + FC) \times EPF \times CGF \times MAF}{2/B \times D} = \text{rating}$$

where L is length, S is sail area, B x D is beam x depth, DC is draft allowance, FC is freeboard allowance, EPF is a factor for the engine and propeller, CGF is the stability factor, and MAF a factor for movable keel surfaces.

Recently, two much simpler systems have been introduced to avoid the complexity of the IOR. Neither of these, the Anglo-French Channel Handicap System (CHS) and the American IMS, has yet been fully adopted internationally.

Sailors were a popular subject for cigar-box labels at the beginning of the twentieth century.

Further Reading

Beken of Cowes, Volumes 1 and 2; Cassell, London, 1966 and 1969.

BLYTH, Chay and Maureen, *Innocent Abroad*; Nautical, Lymington, Hampshire, 1970.

BRUCE, Errol, *Cape Horn to Port*; Nautical, Lymington, Hampshire, 1978.

BRYER, Robin, *Jolie Brise*; Secker and Warburg, London, 1982.

CASSON, L., *Illustrated History of Ships and Boats*; Doubleday, New York, 1964.

CHAPELLE, H.I., *The Search for Speed under Sail*; Allen and Unwin, London, 1968.

CHICHESTER, F., *The Lonely Sea and the Sky*; Hodder and Stoughton, London, 1964.
    Gypsy Moth Circles the Globe; World Books, London, 1967.

CLARKE, D.H., *An Evolution in Singlehanders*; Stanford Maritime, London, 1976.

DEAR, I., DAY, G., and McCORMICK H., *Out There*; Seven Seas, Newport, R.I., 1983.

EASTLAND, J., *Great Yachts and Their Designers*; Adlard Coles, London, 1987.

FISHER, B., *The Greatest Race*; Robertsbridge, London, 1986.
    12 Metre Images; Pelham, London, 1986.

FISHER, B., and ROSS, B., *The America's Cup*; Arum, London, 1987.

FOX, Uffa, *More Joys of Living*; Nautical, Lymington, Hampshire.

GRUBB, F.E., *The Venturesome Voyage of Captain Voss*; Gray's Publishing, Winnipeg, 1976.

GUZZWELL, J., *Trekka Round the World*; McKay, New York, 1979.

HISCOCK, E.C., *Cruising Under Sail*; Oxford University Press, 1950.

KENNY, R., *To Win the Admiral's Cup*; Nautical, Lymington, Hampshire, 1974.

KING, B., *Capsize*; Nautical, Lymington, Hampshire, 1969.
    Adventure in Depth; Nautical, Lymington, Hampshire, 1975.

KNIGHT, E.F., *The Cruise on the Alerte*; Grafton, London, 1987.

KNOX-JOHNSTON, R., *A World of My Own*; Grafton, London, 1988.
    Last but not Least; Angus and Robertson, Brighton, 1978.

LEVITT & LLOYD, *Upset, Australia wins the America's Cup*; Nautical Quarterly Publications, New York, 1983.

MIDDLETON, E.E., *The Cruise of the Kate*; Grafton, London, 1986.

MILNES-WALKER, N., *When I put out to Sea*; Collins, London, 1972.

McMULLEN, *Down Channel*, Grafton, London, 1986.

MOITESSIER, B., *Sailing to the Reefs*, Hollis and Carter, London, 1970.
    Cape Horn, the Logical Route; Adlard Coles, London, 1969.

O'BRIEN, Conor, *Across Three Oceans*, Grafton, London, 1987.

PAGE, Frank, *Alone across the Atlantic*, The Observer, London, 1980.

PICKTHALL, B., *The Ultimate Challenge*; Orbis, London, 1983.

PICKTHALL, B. and KNOX-JOHNSTON, R., *The BOC Challenge, 1976/77*; Robertsbridge, London, 1987.

ROSE, Alec, *My Lively Lady*; Nautical, Lymington, Hampshire, 1968.

ROTH, Hal, *The Longest Race*; Norton, New York, 1983.

SLOCUM, J., *Sailing Alone Around the World*; Hart Davis, London, 1948.

SMEETON, Miles, *Once is Enough*; Grafton, London, 1986.
    Sunrise to Windward; Grafton, London, 1987.

TETLEY, N., *Trimaran Solo*; Nautical, Lymington, Hampshire, 1970.

TILMAN, H.W., *Mischief amongst the Penguins*; Grafton, London, 1988.

TOMALIN and HALL, *The Strange Last Voyage of Donald Crowhurst*; Hodder and Stoughton, London, 1970.

WELD, Phil, *Moxie*; Little Brown, Canada, 1972.

Index

The model room at the New York Yacht Club. Over the years members have supplied half-models of their yachts to make this magnificent collection.